THE SECRET POWER OF DREAMS

Professor David Fontana is a psychologist who holds posts in the University of Wales, Cardiff, and the University of Minho, Portugal. He is the author of 16 books which have been translated into 19 languages and has been lecturing and running workshops on dreams for some years. David Fontana has also had extensive experience in broadcasting on the subject of dreams for national television and radio.

THE SECRET
POWER OF DREAMS

A New Approach to Unlocking Their Hidden Potential

DAVID FONTANA

ELEMENT
Shaftesbury, Dorset ● Rockport, Massachusetts
Brisbane, Queensland

© David Fontana 1990, 1995

Originally published as *Dreamlife*

First published in Great Britain in 1995 by
Element Books Limited
Shaftesbury, Dorset SP7 8BP

Published in the USA in 1995 by
Element Books, Inc.
PO Box 830, Rockport, MA 01966

Published in Australia in 1995 by
Element Books Limited
for Jacaranda Wiley Limited
33 Park Road, Milton, Brisbane 4064

Cover design by Max Fairbrother
Page design by Roger Lightfoot
Typeset by ABM Typographics Limited
Printed and bound in Great Britain by
Hartnolls Limited, Bodmin, Cornwall

British Library Cataloguing in Publication
data available

Library of Congress Cataloging in Publication Data
Fontana, David
[Dreamlife]
The secret power of dreams: a new approach to unlocking
their hidden potential/David Fontana.
Includes bibliographical references and index.
1. Dreams. 2. Dream interpretation. I. Title.
BF 1091. F 66 1995
154.6′ 3–dc20 95–12180

ISBN 1–85230–697–1

CONTENTS

With love and thanks to
my brother Kenneth,
who also cares about dreams

INTRODUCTION

It is hard to imagine a more evocative opening sentence to a story than that used by Daphne du Maurier in her novel *Rebecca*, 'Last night I dreamt I went to Manderley again'. 'Last night I dreamt . . .'. The words speak directly to our imagination because in dreams we enter into the world of the imagination, an altered state of awareness in which we trade everyday reality for a strange world full of infinite possibilities. A world in which the past, the future, the present, lose their boundaries. Sometimes in this world we appear much as we are now, sometimes as we were years ago, sometimes as we may be in the years to come. Magical landscapes open up before us, arising and dissolving as if at the wish of an enchanter. Familiar people act in weird, unfamiliar ways. Unknown people appear and we greet them as if we have always known them. Bizarre adventures unwind before us, with ourselves sometimes as actors and sometimes as spectators. In dreams we fly, we make war, we make love, we exercise incredible powers.

Dreams and Waking Life

Few people are unmoved by the subject of dreams. Dreams captivate us because of their refusal to be bound by the laws of waking life, because of their trick of turning wishes into reality, of taking us into a story instead of leaving us to experience it from the outside. Dreams turn us into magicians. They intrigue, they inspire. We wonder why they arise and what they are for. We marvel at their creative power, at the vividness of their imagery, at the way they far outdistance the things our imagination can produce in waking life.

At times, they even seem to represent a parallel existence, another life influenced by, yet distinct from, our waking experiences. Another life which we enter each night in the hours of sleep, not choosing our journey, caught up in it as if sometimes we are characters in another person's fantasy, actors in another person's drama. Dreams dissolve the boundaries of normality, they challenge the way in which we see and think about the world, they show us that life may indeed be other than what we think it to be.

In a sense, dreams can outweigh even the most moving experience art or books or theatre can give us, because even the greatest drama demands of us that we suspend our disbelief. In dreams there is no such demand, because in many dreams there *is* no disbelief. However fantastic the dream events are to our waking minds, our dreaming self accepts them without question. We walk into a room we know each day of our waking lives and find it strangely altered, yet the dreaming self bats not a dreaming eyelid. We pick up a cup and it changes into a gun, we meet a friend and his face becomes that of an enemy, we run and our legs refuse to carry us, then moments later we are moving faster than a galloping horse. We jump over rooftops. We commit incredible acts of folly and incredible acts of bravery. Nothing is implausible, nothing is incongruous. The dream makes its own rules, and we accept these rules as if they are the rules of existence itself.

In the language of waking life, dreams are used as synonyms for states of great success or happiness. 'It worked like a dream,' we say. 'I had to pinch myself to make sure I wasn't dreaming.' 'I never dreamt it could be so wonderful.' 'Even in my wildest dreams I never imagined....' 'You're my dream lover.' 'It's always been my dream to....' 'I used to dream about days like this.' And so on. Dreams are our way of upgrading mundane reality. In referring to this mundane reality, Omar Khayyam (in Fitzgerald's inspired translation) speaks for most of us when he says:

Ah love, could thou and I with Fate conspire
To grasp this sorry Scheme of Things entire,
Would not we shatter it to bits – and then
Remould it nearer to the Heart's Desire!

Well, in dreams we can remould it. Once we enter their mysterious world we can indeed grasp the sorry scheme of things which waking life sometimes represents, and remake it closer to how we would have it be.

Should we, in spite of this, still doubt the power of dreams, it is as well to remind ourselves that dreams intrude into waking life more emphatically than waking life intrudes into dreams. We may view our dreams as flimsy, fragile things that fade in the moment of waking, yet in dreams waking life is even more flimsy and fragile. It is customary in waking life to remember our dreams, yet rare in dreams to recall the events of waking life. And although waking life provides the raw material for our dreams, dreams can also provide the raw material for waking life, sometimes in particularly spectacular and epoch-making ways (see Chapter 3).

And yet, and yet. . . . For there is a qualification, and an important one, to be set against these positive aspects of dreaming. It is that dreams can disturb as well as excite, terrify as well as delight. For if dreams make their own rules, then there is no safety for us in them. A pursuer can pass through a wall as easily as we can. He or she can intrude into the securest of sanctuaries. In dreams there is no guarantee of privacy, no guarantee of good triumphing over evil, no guarantee of escape. Our gun can turn back into a cup just when we have most need of it, or it can spit out bullets to which our pursuers are impervious. Our friends can turn against us. Our legs can refuse to carry us, our voice can refuse to speak, our body can refuse to move. A strong swimmer, we can find ourselves sinking like a stone in shallow water. A diligent student, we can find ourselves sitting an exam for which we are ludicrously unprepared. Used to exercising authority and leadership, we can find ourselves in our dream totally without power. Popular and well-liked we can find ourselves a lamentable figure of fun. Modest and even prudish we can find ourselves naked in public. A happy parent we can find ourselves grieving for our lost children.

For the dream can take away from us as readily as it gives. It can trick us, deceive us, menace us, fill us with such fear or sadness that the memory shakes us for days and even years to come. No matter how far-fetched the dream, the emotions it arouses can haunt us for half a lifetime. They can threaten our security, disturb our peace, unsettle our picture of ourselves and of others. They can alarm us to the point where we feel terrified to re-enter sleep, can come between us and our work and our relationships, can remind us of our mortality and of the mortality of those we love and of the things we cherish.

So 'Last night I dreamt I went to Manderley again' can have its bad side as well as its good. Our personal Manderley may be lit with joy or shrouded in gloom, may be peopled with angels or peopled with demons, may entice or repel, may bring us hope or bring us despair. To add to the confusion, we may find ourselves powerless to predict which of these opposites it is going to be. Sometimes during a happy phase in our lives our dreams may be filled with foreboding and menace. At other times, when our waking life is depressed and negative, our dream life may be bright with optimism and hope. Try as we might, we may find it hard to see a link between our waking and our sleeping lives, between who I think I am and who my dreams think I am. And in the end, perhaps, find it hard to decide which of them represents the real me.

Dreams and the Creative Mind

It's little wonder therefore that across the centuries dreams have taken such a hold upon the popular imagination. From the beginning of recorded history people have discussed their dreams, written about them, searched them for meaning, drawn pictures of them. They have woven them into the fabric of many of their most enduring myths and legends, built around them gripping tales for children, drawn from them the inspiration for great works in both art and science. They have used them as warnings of disaster, as ways of seeing into the future. The Bible and some of the other great spiritual books of mankind are full of them. God speaks to men and women in dreams. In both the Old and the New Testament they have a crucial role in shaping history.

In the Old Testament, for example, Joseph became rich and powerful by virtue of his understanding and interpretation of dreams, while the New Testament Joseph was 'warned of God in a dream' about dangers to the infant Christ. Pilate's wife cautioned Pilate to do nothing against Christ 'for I have suffered many things this day in a dream because of him'. In the Old Testament, God told Aaron and Miriam that if there was a true prophet among the Israelites 'I...will speak unto him in a dream', while Job announced that 'when deep sleep falleth upon men... then He openeth the ears of men and sealeth their instruction'. In Islam, it is accepted that God can speak to men and women 'in the form of sights or visions when the qualified recipient is asleep or in a state of trance.' (Abdalati, *Islam in Focus*, 1978).

The Buddhists, the Hindus, the ancient Egyptians and the ancient Greeks all prized the messages received in dreams. Both the *Odyssey* and the *Aeneid* refer to the Greek belief in the gate of ivory and the gate of horn, with true dreams issuing through the former and false dreams through the latter. Socrates throughout his life had a recurring dream 'appearing in different forms and at different times, but always saying the same thing, "Socrates, practise and cultivate the arts" '. In Aborigine myths the world was created in the *dream time*, while in the shamanic culture that once flourished throughout much of Asia and still survives in certain Tibetan Buddhist and American Indian practices, dreams and trance were thought to allow the adept to receive knowledge of the future and of distant events, and to leave his or her body and travel in the spirit realms.

And should we attempt to dismiss all this as evidence of the working of superstitious or of primitive minds, it is well to remind ourselves of the number of scientists in more modern times who confess that the inspiration for their work came to them in dreams. So extensive and so significant is the evidence they provide that it deserves, along with a look at the part dreams have played in artistic creativity, a section to itself. So I shall return to it in Chapter 3. But for the moment the clear message is that both in religion and in science (two areas which some would regard as at opposite ends of human experience) dreams have the ability to provide information that can be used productively and accurately to influence the things that are done in waking life.

So closely linked, in a sense, are our dreaming and our waking lives that it is hardly surprising that great literature abounds in accounts of dreams, and many of the finest plots have dreams or visions as their setting or as part of their action, from John Bunyan's *Pilgrim's Progress* to Charles Dickens' *Christmas Carol*, from Lewis Caroll's *Alice in Wonderland* to William Shakespeare's *Macbeth*. One of the earliest poems in the English language, *The Dream of the Rood*, relates the poet's dream-like experience of the crucifixion and the resurrection, and of the joys and sufferings of the souls in heaven and hell. Many modern novelists and even more writers of children's books find the dream irresistible as a way of setting their plots or of extricating themselves from episodes in their stories which have become a little too fantastic and unreal. The assumptions behind their use of dreams is that we all take dreams seriously enough to be able to identify with the adventures and emotions of the fictional dreamer, and that this identification will help to start and hold our imagination.

Scepticism and Gullibility About Dreams

But once more I have to say 'and yet and yet....'. For in spite of the evidence, many scientists in the academic disciplines of biology and psychology refuse to believe in the fact that the *content* of dreams is of importance. Whilst accepting that dreaming may have a useful function – in, for example, dumping unwanted material from our memory store – they see nothing in the actual content of dreams beyond the result of the confusing firing of electrical brain signals. Certain scientists even counsel that any attempt to remember our dreams is directly counter-productive, and analogous to storing garbage instead of allowing the refuse-men to take it away.

Their arguments are examined in Chapter 1. Diametrically opposed to them are the arguments of people who find it all too easy to read deep significance into the simplest of dreams, to cling to the idea that the dream is always full of special meaning, an infallible guide to inner truths inaccessible by other means. Like an audience listening open-mouthed to travellers' tales, the tendency here is to place dreams on a plane above normal mental functioning, and to see working on your dreams as an easy alternative to working on your everyday life.

These two orientations, the sceptical scientific on the one hand and the over-gullible on the other, are the Scylla and Charybdis between which a more properly objective approach to the phenomenon of dreaming is (sometimes precariously) poised. Such an approach sees dream content as neither on a par with the other waste material of our throwaway society, nor as invariably conveying some form of higher wisdom sent to us by forces which know our own business much better than we do. The aim of this book is to present this approach.

In doing so, I shall look at what we really know about dreams and what we only think we know. And I shall discuss how we can learn from our dreams, and how we can work to make this learning more focused and to improve its quality. But one word of warning. Just as dreams themselves are a voyage into the unknown, so in a way is any book about them. Beware therefore of authors who claim to give you final answers. Beware of dream dictionaries which claim to interpret your dreams for you, or of books which give you techniques for working with your dreams that are the same for each dreamer and for each dream. Dreams operate on many different levels, and often in different ways for different people. In the end, the only person who can fully interpret your dreams for you is you yourself. The aim of this book is to put you in a better position to do this interpreting.

At the end of *The Tempest*, Shakespeare speaks of the 'cloud capped towers, the gorgeous palaces, the solemn temples, the great globe itself' as dissolving like an insubstantial pageant. They are 'such stuff as dreams are made of'. And just as Shakespeare's creation of the dream world of his plays was an intensely personal thing, given breath and life and meaning only by his own genius, so are our dreams our own creation, each man and woman to their own. Just as no simple formula would encompass the genius of a Shakespeare, so no simple formula can encompass the genius of our dreaming. Each of us creates and must understand his or her own dreams at a personal level. There are landmarks, signposts to this understanding, but essentially it must come from each one of us, in our own time and in our own way. This book is a set of such landmarks, such signposts, no more and no less. Its job is to point you on your way. But it cannot do your travelling for you. That is – and will always remain – your own task.

To end the chapter on a personal note; I cannot remember a time when I was not fascinated by dreams, my own and other people's. As a boy I never really pondered their meaning, I simply enjoyed them (with the exception of one nightmare so vivid I still recall its sinister, chilling impact). However, during my early training as a psychologist I soon read enough to discover that there was much more to dreams than simple enjoyment, important as this is, and from then on I have used dreams extensively as a way of finding out more about the human mind. Listening to other people's dreams in therapy and in dream workshops, I have found that they can often get us to the root of a psychological problem much more quickly than any other method. Equally importantly, I have seen how remembering and talking about one's dreams, and starting to take them more seriously, often opens up a new dimension in people's lives. Through the exercise of dream recall and dream analysis, you come to know yourself better, to recognise better your own hidden depths, to marvel more and more at the creative power of your own mind. If this book can help to open up this new dimension for you, the reader, then I will be as pleased about it as you.

1

DREAMING, THE BRAIN
AND THE BODY

Let's start by looking at modern scientific methods of studying dreams. Although these methods don't necessarily bring us closer to understanding what dreams are for or to understanding the origin and meaning of dreams, they tell us a great deal about the incidence and frequency of dreams during the hours of sleep, and about what happens to the physical body when we dream. By pinpointing the moments during sleep when dreaming is most likely to occur, they also allow us to wake people when dreams are taking place, and thus listen to accurate descriptions of the things they're dreaming about. This is a major advance, since dreams, unless we are prepared to take them seriously and start working on them, are notoriously difficult for most people to remember upon normal waking.

At this scientific level, we've learnt more about dreaming during the last three decades or so than ever before in human history. Most of this learning has been done in what are known as sleep (or dream) laboratories, special rooms where subjects sleep wired up to devices that measure physiological responses such as brain waves, heart beat, blood pressure, muscular activity and eye movements throughout the night. At certain points during the night these responses change in ways which I shall discuss shortly, and if subjects are woken up at these points they almost invariably report dreams.

What Happens When We Sleep?

But before we look at what this work tells us about dreaming, we should look at something of what it tells us about the theatre which forms the setting for our dreams, namely sleep itself. Increasing interest was focused upon sleep research by the discovery that during the night the sleeper experiences four different stages or levels of sleep as measured by brain waves and general physiological activity. (In technical language we can say that the *frequency* of our brain waves decreases from between 4 to 8 cycles per second to between 0.5 to 2 cycles per second, while their *strength* increases from between 50 to 100 microvolts to between 100 to 200.)

Within the first hour of sleep we disengage increasingly from the outside world and descend through the four gradually deepening levels until we reach level four, and what is in many ways our deepest sleep of the night. At this level breathing becomes slow and rhythmic; blood pressure, heart rate and body temperature decrease; physical movement becomes minimal; the electrical activity of the brain changes from its waking state; and bodily metabolism slows down markedly.

Somewhere around one to one and a half hours into sleep the pattern alters, however, and we move back upwards through the levels until we reach level one again. Many of the physiological changes associated with the deep sleep of level four are now reversed. The pulse becomes faster and often irregular, respiration and blood pressure increase, metabolism and brain waves return nearer to their waking state, the body often changes position, and in males penile erection usually takes place. At this point, we seem on the verge of waking, yet paradoxically there is a marked decrease in muscle tone and it is often harder to arouse us now than it is during deep level four sleep, hence the term *paradoxical sleep* which is sometimes used to describe this re-entry into level one sleep. So dissimilar is paradoxical sleep from deep sleep, with each in fact as physiologically distinct from the other as they both are from waking, that some authorities argue we should talk about the three states as three distinct states of being.

A particular characteristic of paradoxical sleep is that, during it, the eyes begin to move rapidly up and down and from side to side behind the closed eyelids. So much so in fact that in sleep

BOX 1
REMEMBERING YOUR DREAMS

The vast majority of us never have the opportunity of going to sleep in a dream laboratory, so we have to find other ways to help us remember and record our dreams. Remembering your dreams is an essential first step in working upon them. Dream research suggests that we all of us dream every night, so, even if up to now you've been unsuccessful in recalling your dreams, it doesn't mean you should fall into the habit of thinking 'I never dream'. With practice and the right techniques, you should soon be able regularly to remember at least one and probably more dreams every morning. (When working intensively on my dreams my own average is around five or six; I don't think this is in any way exceptional.)

To remember your dreams, practise the following:

1. Take your dreams seriously. The *motivation* to remember your dreams is a vital first step.

2. Whenever you think of it, tell yourself during the day that you will remember the dreams you have that night. Don't try and 'force' this message on yourself. Simply state it as a matter of fact.

3. As you lie in bed preparing for sleep, repeat the message over and over. If this keeps you awake, decide on a certain number of repetitions (say 12), and then stop and compose yourself for sleep.

4. When you wake in the morning (or in the night), don't change your physical position in bed. Stay just as you are.

5. Concentrate on the thoughts running through your head and/or upon the emotions you may be feeling. Hold them at the centre of your awareness. Often they will trigger off dream memories.

6. Keep a notebook or a tape recorder by the bed, and write down these memories before they fade (see also page 20). Use the *present tense* when doing so. This helps recall (particularly of emotions and feelings), and makes the dream experience more relevant and immediate.

7. Return to the dream memories as often as possible during the day, so that you can 're-enter' the dream much as you would a waking memory.

8. Don't become discouraged or impatient. Keep trying. It may take days or weeks, but success will come.

BOX 1
REMEMBERING YOUR DREAMS

If you want a short-cut to success, set your alarm to go off three hours or so after the time you usually fall asleep. This usually coincides with the second period of REM sleep, so you are likely to wake in the middle of a dream. If this doesn't work, experiment by moving the alarm forward or backwards 15 minutes or so each night until you hit the right time.

laboratories this movement can be observed even without sleep monitoring equipment, simply by watching the person as he or she enters this state. These rapid eye movements give para-doxical sleep its more usual title of *rapid eye movement* or REM sleep (another term for it is *emergent sleep*; levels two to four are usually referred to as NREM or non-rem sleep), and it is in fact the onset of our first major nightly episode of dreaming. On some 80 per cent of the occasions when aroused at this point, subjects report vivid dreams. Normally, this first stage of REM sleep lasts no more than five to ten minutes, after which the subject sinks once more into deeper sleep (though usually without reaching beyond level two or level three sleep at any time during the remainder of the night).

Subsequently NREM and REM sleep alternate with each other in approximately one to two hour cycles throughout the night, with usually some four to seven repetitions of the cycle. Each of the deep sleep states is progressively shallower (we may only reach the depth of level four sleep during the first period of NREM sleep), while each of the REM states is progressively longer, culminating in the longest period (twenty to forty minutes) just before waking. The average adult spends around one and a half hours in REM sleep each night, though this may decrease to around one and a quarter hours in old age (when level four sleep also decreases and may even disappear altogether). Newborn babies pass a great deal of their lives in this state (some 60 per cent of their total sleeping time), while, interestingly, premature babies pass even more (up to 70 per cent).

During the early years of scientific sleep research (the 1950s and 1960s) it was thought that all our dreaming takes place during REM sleep. We now know that this is not the case. Some 50 per cent or so of subjects roused during NREM sleep also report dreams, but these are of a different kind from REM dreams. During REM sleep, dreams are vivid and active (the typical magic picture-show that we associate with dreaming), whereas in NREM sleep around 40 per cent of subjects report what seem more like shadowy, indistinct thoughts, set in a muffled fog-bound world in which dim shapes move in and out of awareness, than real dreams. The remaining 10 per cent report dreams similar to those in REM sleep, although usually shorter, less vivid, less bizarre, and with less physical activity and less emotional content.

Why Do We Sleep?

Disappointingly (though given the materialistic approach of much of modern science some would say not surprisingly), sleep research still hasn't solved the question why we dream *or even why we sleep*. Theories abound. For example a view sometimes put forward is that we sleep to conserve our energy. Another suggestion is that as the hunger mechanism is suppressed during sleep, we sleep in order to conserve food supplies – in other words that sleep is a protective mechanism developed early in man's evolution. Another evolutionary argument is that, as we are at our most vulnerable during the hours of darkness, sleep (and the death-like drop in bodily metabolism that sleep brings) renders us less likely to be selected as a tasty meal by nocturnal animals. A more psychological explanation has it that, as our learning processes are largely inactivated during sleep, this gives the brain a chance to reorganise and store more efficiently the information gathered during the day.

These theories apart, sleep is certainly a pleasant and relaxing experience for the great majority of us, and a logical explanation would therefore be that it's there to help the body recuperate physically. However, there's no unequivocal physiological or chemical evidence from research that this is the case (from research with human beings that is; there is evidence of death in rats after four weeks of continuous sleep deprivation in the laboratory – doubtless because they found death a preferable alternative to co-operating any longer with experiments of such mindless cruelty).

Certainly people will literally pass out on their feet if they're deprived of sleep for too long. But there are plenty of instances of individuals who can manage with very little sleep. And there is at least one case in the scientific literature of a man who, after a medical problem, claimed to find sleep of any kind impossible. (Over a four-night period in the sleep laboratory he did appear – according to the equipment monitoring his brain waves – to take one spell of sleep, but it lasted only minutes and afterwards he confessed himself totally unaware it had taken place.) Also, as I shall discuss in Chapter 8, certain spiritually advanced men and women claim to remain conscious throughout the night, so whether they can really be said to sleep or not is a moot point.

Physiologically and chemically then, apart from the fact that some children seem to secrete more growth hormone during sleep than during waking hours, any changes that are observed during sleep seem to have relatively little to do with actual physical renewal. In fact deep meditation can in some subjects produce more relaxation and greater changes in bodily metabolism than can even the most profound sleep. But research shows that irritability, anxiety and poor concentration all increase dramatically after the loss of only one or two nights' sleep, which certainly points to sleep as having an important *psychological* function for the vast majority of us. A function which can perhaps be replaced by deep meditational states, but only in those rare individuals who are able, through training, motivation and long practice, to attain these states.

Also of interest is the fact that the brain produces less of two chemicals called serotonin and noradrenaline during sleep (and perhaps particularly during REM sleep). Both serotonin and noradrenaline play a part in the transmission of nerve impulses in the brain, and their reduction means that the body is less able to transmit external signals to the brain (which may be one reason why in REM sleep we are particularly difficult to arouse). Even more importantly, serotonin and noradrenaline may be involved in the control of body temperature and in such higher-order functions as attention and learning. So sleep could be there in order to give the brain a rest from producing these chemicals, and thus to allow it to be more refreshed and aler when it resumes full activity upon waking. Or, just as likely, the opposite could be the case, and the production of serotonin and noradrenaline could be decreased in order to allow us to sleep.

Which of these particular viewpoints you support is very much a matter of individual choice. But since serotonin is also thought to suppress hallucinations, it is intriguing to argue that the reduction at least in serotonin during sleep is a deliberate move by the body to enhance our capacity to experience the hallucinations of dreaming. Which lends support to the second of them. And suggests an even more intriguing argument, namely that perhaps we sleep partly *in order to dream*. Sleep, in other words, may be the servant of the dream.

Is there any other evidence to support this argument? Some laboratory experiments do in fact show that if we are deprived of sleep, we spend an increased amount of time in REM sleep on subsequent nights, as if it's more important to catch up on REM than on NREM. Experiments also show that if we stop people experiencing REM by waking them each time they reach this level, they have to be roused more and more frequently as the nights go by. So there's strong evidence we need REM sleep, and probably the dreaming that goes with it.

It's hardly surprising therefore that the ancients supported the view that sleep was there for the purposes of dreaming. And dreaming, they concluded, was there for the purposes of allowing us to enter another world. In most occult and early spiritual traditions, something (the consciousness, the soul, the astral body – terms for it vary) leaves the body during sleep and is free to travel in this other world, fragmentary memories of which it brings back in the form of dreams. Modern research into Out-of-the-Body Experiences (OBEs) and into Near-Death Experiences (NDEs) provide some support for the idea that a part at least of our consciousness may leave us during sleep and again at the moment of death, a finding which has interesting implications for the material I cover in Chapter 8.

ly, many 'orthodox' scientists remain uninter-
h into OBEs and NDEs, and into such, to them,
.... as a part of the consciousness leaving the body.
For them, even human consciousness (except possibly their
own) is of relatively minor importance. Since there is no good
scientific way in which consciousness can be explained
(evolutionary theories are at a loss to account for it; in
evolutionary terms there's no good reason why consciousness
should ever have developed at all, and no mechanism to explain
how it could have done so), they prefer to regard it as a kind of
biological accident. A by-product of more important biological
functioning, just as noise is a by-product of the working of
machines such as petrol engines and spin-dryers.

If such orthodox scientists have no final answer to the riddle
of consciousness or to the question of why we sleep, it's not
surprising they have no final answer either to the question of
why we dream. The theories they put forward can be grouped
under three main headings, and I'll look quickly at each in turn.
We can call them respectively the *neuro-physiological model, the
learning/remembering model,* and the *forgetting model.*

The neuro-physiological model of dreaming suggests that during
REM sleep the brain stem spontaneously generates signals
which stimulate sensory channels in the brain much as input
from the senses stimulates them in waking life. The brain
elaborates these signals into visual and auditory images, a kind
of *sensory mimicry* which tricks the sleeper into believing he is
having real experiences – in other words which tricks him into
experiencing dreams. Since in sleep we are deprived of
regularising and stabilising information from outside our heads
against which we can test our dream events, we accept these
events as 'real', no matter how outrageous they may be. And
outrageous they certainly are, since the signals generated in
sleep by the brain stem are random and confused, unlike the
ordered events presented to us by the waking world.

The physiological model also suggests that, since the
production of serotonin and noradrenaline is reduced during
sleep, the brain processes information in a more confused way,

and we thus lose in dreams our sense of self-awareness and of critical judgement.

The neuro-physiological model is all right as far as it goes, but as an explanation of dreaming – as opposed simply to an account of the neuro-physiological activity that accompanies dreaming – it makes the mistake (all too common in orthodox science) of confusing *process* with *cause*. That is, it may describe accurately enough the process which goes on in the brain during dreaming, but it does nothing to explain what causes this process in the first place and why it is there at all – in other words, what sets it off and the reason for its existence. This confusion is rather like saying that since the engine is the mechanical device that powers the automobile, it must therefore also be the driver.

The model further fails to tell us why dreams contain such a strong narrative content. For all their bizarre nature, dreams are not a succession of incoherent, disconnected events, as we would expect if they were explicable solely in terms of the spontaneous firing of neurological signals in the brain stem. On the contrary, dreams tell stories. The events they contain show development one from another, and often carry a clear thread of apparent meaning. Dream events hang together, and do so in a way hard to account for simply in terms of spontaneous neurological activity.

The Learning/Remembering Model is really an extension of the neuro-physiological model in that it advances a reason why the brain stem fires off its signals in REM sleep. This reason is that these signals activate higher areas of the brain and in doing so maintain and reinforce learnt material which has been stored in our memory during waking life, rather as going over and over this material in the day maintains and reinforces it. They may also give the neurons and electrical circuits in the brain an opportunity to practise even during the hours of sleep. Our dreams are the subjective experience of this reinforcement and maintenance activity.

The first objection to this model is that it is purely speculative. There is no hard evidence to back it up. But the second and more important objection is that dreams seem to go way beyond a repeated and wearisome rehearsal of the events of waking life. And when they do relate to these events, they often transform, elaborate and distort them in a way that is likely to confuse rather than to reinforce and maintain waking memory. As I suggested in the Introduction and as I shall discuss more fully in Chapter 3, dreams in fact function *creatively*, and I shall return to this point in a moment after discussing the third main group of explanations for dreaming advanced by orthodox science.

The Forgetting Model argues that REM sleep serves to remove unwanted data from the memory. So many things happen to us during the day that if we remembered them all our brains would soon become like a chocked lumber room, far too full to allow us to find anything we want or to allow us space to store any new bits of information that we really do need to remember.

Rather like a computer dumping unwanted programmes, the mind therefore in sleep reduces (perhaps through the diminished output of our old friends the neurotransmitters serotonin and noradrenaline) the strength between brain neurons, thus allowing information to be lost. The sleeping mind experiences this dumping process in the form of dreams, but in fact it is not really intended for our attention at all.

The forgetting model therefore gives us a reason why dreams are so hard to remember (we're not intended to remember them in the first place). Further, it suggests that it is probably harmful to make any attempt to remember them, because such an attempt is like hanging onto our household rubbish instead of allowing the refuse-men to take it away. In support of this suggestion it is sometimes argued that work with people interned in concentration camps during World War II shows that some individuals who rarely remember dreams of any kind (even when woken during REM sleep) have adjusted better to the memory of their terrible experiences than have those who frequently report dreams, many of which still relate back to these experiences.

This is of course very much a chicken and egg argument. Is it because people who dump their dreams dump their unwanted experiences, or is it because people who have dumped their unwanted experiences no longer need to dream about them? As we shall see in Chapter 2, Perls for example sees dreams as reflecting unfinished emotional material. So the tendency of concentration camp victims to dream about experiences that are still very much on their minds is exactly what we would expect, just as is the tendency of those who have come to terms with these experiences to stop dreaming about them.

A further objection to this argument is that in any case it is dangerous to generalise from certain very special cases to the population at large. There is no evidence that in this population people who remember their dreams are less psychologically healthy than people who don't. Many psychologists in fact maintain that the weight of evidence points emphatically in the opposite direction.

But an even more important objection, this time to both the neuro-physiological model and to the forgetting model, is that dreams – as I suggested in the Introduction and as I shall discuss more fully in Chapter 3 – are able to function creatively. That is, *they are able to go beyond the information given.* Far from providing essentially random and confused material (the neuro-physiological model) or unwanted rubbish from the day's experiences (the forgetting model) they can provide new solutions to old problems, can offer new avenues for creative expression in waking life, and can help us reflect more deeply upon waking experiences.

So compelling is the evidence for dream creativity that one suspects that proponents of the three models we've just discussed can surely not have studied it. One suspects also that they are unlikely to have studied their own dreams. In fact, by their faith in their own arguments, champions of the forgetting model expressly discourage themselves from so doing. Their contention that it is counter-productive to remember one's own dreams dooms them to disregard the very evidence that would undermine their model – hardly a very scientific way of proceeding.

On a purely personal note, I find that when meditating (the relationship between meditation and dreaming is explored on page 128) I often reach a level where suddenly and spontaneously I recall a string of dreams, some of which I am certain I have not remembered before in waking life. This indicates that all the material concerned is stored somewhere in the mind and for some good purpose.

BOX 2
KEEPING A DREAM DIARY

You will need to keep a dream diary if you want to work on your dreams. A dream diary is like a daily diary except that in it you record your sleeping instead of your waking adventures. I said in Box 1 (page 11) that you should keep paper and pencil by the side of your bed and record your dreams upon awaking, and this is the first stage in your dream diary. Use a notebook, and put a date against each dream.

But what kind of detail should you include in your dream diary? The answer is, the more detail the better. As you gain practice and train yourself in dream recall, you will find more and more details come back to you. Write them down. They may be important when it comes to the later business of analysing your dreams. Don't start off with any one theory of what dreams 'mean' too firmly entrenched in your mind. Such a theory can lead you to ignore as of no value things which may in fact turn out to be very significant.

When keeping your dream diary, in particular:

* Write down the dream events in their proper order. This may seem unimportant if the events appear unrelated to each other. But once you begin the process of analysis, relationships often become very clear.

* Keep a careful note of the dream characters. Who was in your dream and what did he or she do? If they remind you of someone you know in waking life, write this down. Don't trust to memory.

* If well-known scenery appears, record any differences between it and the same scenery in waking life. Were the doors/windows in the right place? Were the colours accurate? Was the size right? And so on. (This is particularly important if you want to develop lucid dreaming – Chapter 7).

* Similarly, record any differences between well-known people in the dream and in real life.

* Record any non-human characters that appeared in the dream (animals, angels) or any inanimate objects that behaved as if alive.

* Make a special note of any *recurring* events, themes or characters. Do they always occur/behave in exactly the same way?

* Note down all the colours you see.

BOX 2
KEEPING A DREAM DIARY

  * Note down your emotional responses to everything.

Finally, don't trust to memory. When you read back over your dream diary you may find you have no recollection at all of having some of the dreams. However clear they seem at the time, *write them down.*

How do I know that what I am recalling are dreams? The answer to this is another question. How do we know the morning after, that what we recall are dreams? This is difficult to test scientifically, but the subjective certainty is unmistakable.

The Mystery of Dreaming Still Remains

So orthodox scientific research, while telling us a great deal about what goes on physiologically and chemically in the brain and in the body generally during sleep and dreaming, leaves us with the overriding conclusion that both these states are still very mysterious indeed. So mysterious in fact that, if one stood back and pondered the matter objectively, it is rather strange that we abandon ourselves to them every night so gratefully and so unthinkingly. Questions as to what on earth is going to happen to us after we've drifted off into sleep, and as to whether or not we are going to wake up in the morning with the same consciousness and the same identity with which we went to sleep, never enter our heads.

Perhaps no traveller ever set off more blithely or with less preparation into the unknown than most of us set off each night into sleep. It was Hamlet who spoke apprehensively of the dreams that might come to haunt us in the sleep of death, and that it was indeed the fear of these dreams that makes us cling to life. He might almost as readily have spoken of the dreams that come to haunt us in the sleep between sunset and sunrise. Alternatively he might have spoken of both sets of dreams with anticipation and excitement. One thing is clear. We probably aren't all that much closer to providing the final answer to their mystery than were men and women in Shakespeare's own time.

Some Conceptions and Misconceptions About Dreaming

However, the findings of orthodox science about dreaming do help us dismiss or support a number of the popular ideas that surround this mysterious state. It's appropriate to conclude this chapter by looking at some of them.

Some people never dream. We've already disposed of this one. It's true to say that some people never *remember* their dreams, but highly unlikely that there are people about who don't dream at all. All the evidence suggests that we all of us dream every night, and that our dreaming follows a relatively set pattern. Even people who claim they have never dreamt in their lives report dreams when they're woken up in sleep laboratories at the appropriate times.

We dream only with the right side of our brains. The brain is divided into two hemispheres, connected by a bundle of nerve fibres at the centre. We know that the left side (which through a cross-over effect controls the *right* side of the body) is concerned mainly with verbal, rational and analytical thinking, while the right side (which controls the left) is more concerned with intuition, imagery, and synthetic thinking. A common belief is that dreaming comes from the right side of the brain, hence its non-rational (and perhaps mystical) nature. However, studies with patients with right hemisphere impairment show they still dream. The left hemisphere does therefore have access to dreaming, though the dreams concerned tend to be unimaginative, utilitarian, more tied to reality and less symbolic than usual.

Some people dream only in black and white. If this is true, it's hard to explain. Colour is a dominant factor in our lives, and there's no obvious reason why the dreaming mind should choose to ignore it. Some surveys show that far more people claim to dream in black and white than in colour, but the truth is probably that such people *forget* the colour in their dreams more quickly than they forget other details. In sleep laboratories people aroused during dreaming almost always report some memory of colour, however hazy.

This isn't to say that we never dream in black and white. I can only remember one black and white dream in my life, but it was a peculiarly vivid one, and the memory of it has persisted strongly over the years. A well-liked friend and colleague died suddenly and tragically, and the night after her death I had a dream of her walking away from me through a sunlit wood carpeted with flowers. If any dream called out for colour that one did, yet my unmistakable memory of it on waking was that it was in black and white. Perhaps the dream was intended to carry a particular significance, and the contrast between it and my usually very colourful dreams was one way of emphasising this. The experience certainly demonstrated to me that black and white dreaming does occur, if only rarely.

The events in dreams may seem to take a long time, but the actual dream is over very quickly. We pack a great deal of activity into dreams, mainly because they cut out those long pauses that take place between events in waking life. The dream doesn't waste time. It concentrates upon peak incidents, and the scenes it contains can change swiftly and dramatically. So in this sense time seems to be speeded up in dreams as compared to normal experience. But in real terms, dream adventures take as long to work themselves through as it would take you to imagine them in your waking life. And research shows that the episodes of dreaming can in fact be quite lengthy, anything up to forty minutes or more in some cases.

Animals don't dream. We can't be sure one way or another, but all the mammals so far monitored during sleep go through those physiological changes associated in humans with dreaming. They may also move their paws as if running, and growl and whimper as if experiencing dream adventures. So the evidence suggests they're dreaming, which raises more questions about the purpose of dreaming than it answers.

Babies don't dream. Again we can't be sure. But babies do in fact spend a very large part of their sleeping hours in REM sleep. As they grow older, the ratio of REM sleep to NREM sleep actually decreases. So babies would seem to be dreaming, though what on earth they are dreaming about is quite another matter.

Dreams never come true. Dreams certainly reflect our waking hopes and fears for the future, and even keeping a cursory record of our dream life shows that (as indeed with daydreams) sometimes these things come about and sometimes they don't. Much may depend upon the ratio between fantasy and reality which we put into our lives. But there may be more to it than this. Can dreams in some way pick up knowledge about future events, even about future events of which we have no current information and therefore no current expectations (for example natural disasters on the other side of the world?). The question must wait until we can explore it at greater length in Chapter 6.

We dream less as we grow older. I've already said that the ratio of REM sleep to NREM sleep is particularly high in babies and declines a little later. But this doesn't mean it goes on declining. We maintain a fairly stable pattern of REM to NREM sleep throughout most of our lives. The slight further decline when old age is reached that I've already mentioned may simply be because sleep patterns themselves tend to change in the elderly, with more naps being taken during the day and fewer hours of sleep at night. If the memory declines in old age, there may also be less tendency to remember dreams. But old people who stick to the sleeping habits of their younger days and stay bright and alert may stick to the same dreaming habits. It's impossible to generalise.

We're more likely to remember those dreams we have just before waking. True. As we've seen, the longest session of REM sleep takes place in the period before waking. It is dreams from this final phase that are most likely to be recalled, though if we wake soon after going to sleep we may remember the dreams from an earlier phase. (Though we'll most likely have forgotten them again by morning.)

You can't control your dreams. People sometimes report dreaming about whatever happens to be on their mind as they're drifting off to sleep. So it's easy to assume you can decide the topic of your dream simply by holding it in your thoughts as sleep overtakes you. You might not be able to decide the direction of the dream, but at least you would be able to decide its setting.

In practice, things aren't as easy as that. You may in fact dream according to plan, but the dream is more likely to happen during your first cycle of dreaming, and not be remembered. Or, in the maddeningly perverse way that dreams have, your dreaming mind may choose to ignore the target altogether in favour of some apparently trivial event that happened earlier in the day. (This is in fact often found to be the case when subjects try to will their dreams during dream research, and are woken during the first dreaming cycle.)

As we'll see later, it's likely that you can gain a degree of control over certain aspects of your dreaming, but the task isn't an easy or a very precise one.

Talking or walking in your sleep indicates bad dreams. It may have done in the case of Lady Macbeth, but that was poetic licence on Shakespeare's part. In actual fact, on being aroused sleep talkers and walkers rarely report they were dreaming, and both talking and walking take place mainly during NREM sleep. Their cause seems to lie in the sporadic firing of speech and motor mechanisms in the brain. The reason this happens in some people and not in others is unknown, but seems to be unrelated to the state of either one's dreaming or of one's conscience. (But all the same, I should still pay more than passing attention to the names your partner calls out in the night, no matter how fast asleep they are.)

You shouldn't try to wake a sleepwalker. As sleepwalking doesn't seem to be connected with dreaming, this point perhaps isn't really relevant, but it often comes up in discussions on dreams. Sleepwalkers can often be quite hard to wake, and understandably they're often very confused and disorientated if they do. So it's better to lead them quietly back to bed if you can. But it's untrue that sleepwalkers never hurt themselves. They can and do, so it's never a good idea to let them get on with their nocturnal rambles (particularly since none of them, in spite of popular belief, has ever been known to lead onlookers to buried treasure).

A big meal just before you go to bed brings on nightmares. Cheese is often advanced as a culprit in this respect. The answer is that a

heavy meal of anything makes the digestion work overtime just
when the whole body should be lowering its metabolism in order
to relax and recuperate. The result, not surprisingly, is a
restless night during which we wake several times, and are
therefore much more aware of our early phases of dreaming
than usual. The following morning we see these dreams as
'caused' by the heavy meal.

But if our full stomach actually leads to stomachache, this
may prompt our dreams to be less pleasant than usual. There's
evidence that the body's physical sensations during the night
can influence dream content. A tight sheet, for example, may
lead to dreams of being tied down, or the breeze from an open
window may lead to dreams of being on the seashore or the
prairies. The moral is a simple one. When we go to bed, our
stomachs want to rest just like the rest of us.

Sleeping on your back causes nightmares. I first read about this one in
a children's encyclopedia when I was a boy. Illustrated by a
graphic picture of a supine child being menaced from a dream
cloud by a feathered Red Indian brandishing a tomahawk, we
young readers were cautioned never to sleep on our backs, and
for some time I earnestly (though I think without much success)
strove to follow this advice. I still wonder how this enduring
myth originated. People certainly snore more often (and more
infuriatingly) when on their backs than when on their sides, but
snoring is as unconnected with dreaming as is sleepwalking.
People sleeping on their backs are also more likely to feel the
pressure of a full bladder. But in any case even the most restful
of sleepers changes position a minimum of eight times during
the night, so we're none of us likely to stay on our backs very
long.

Another myth I first encountered in childhood was that you
should never sleep on your left side as it made your heart swell
up and could kill you. In more recent years I was intrigued to
find that a particular Buddhist order instructs its monks always
to sleep on their right sides, and since Buddhists know a thing
or two I wondered if the myth could have some truth in it after
all, however tenuous. That is until I shortly afterwards came
across another order that instructs its monks to settle to sleep on
their left sides. I'm not sure which order claims to keep their

hearts in the best shape or to have the sweetest dreams.

More people have unpleasant than pleasant dreams. In dream surveys more people do in fact report dreams involving aggressive acts and negative emotions such as anger, fear and sadness than friendly acts and positive emotions such as happiness, calmness and excitement. This may be because people are more inclined to remember negative dreams, or are more anxious to talk about them and get at their meaning. But since the dreaming mind seems to be concerned for much of the time with our waking problems, maybe this is just what we would expect. Dream research shows in addition that depressed people have more depressing dreams and anxious people more anxious dreams than do the rest of the population.

You don't dream when you're drunk. Most drugs reduce the incidence of dreaming, and alcohol is no exception. To date, no drug that reliably *enhances* dreaming has been discovered. Some drugs appear to enrich the hypnagogic state (the state between waking and sleeping – see Chapter 4) in that under their influence the images seen at this time take on a particular vividness and clarity, but whether this is because the drugs prolong this state and thus give us more chance to be aware of it or because they actually change its quality we don't as yet know.

Frequent sex dreams reveal an abnormally high sex drive. It's true we tend to dream more frequently about the things that preoccupy us. And some studies show that sexual offenders have more dreams about violent sex than do the rest of us. So the frequency of our sexual dreams may tell us something about our sex drive. On the other hand they may simply tell us that our sex drive is being frustrated in some way (whether for good reasons or for bad), rather as the frequent dreams about food experienced by the hungry stand as sad testimony to frustrations of a different kind.

In adolescence, sex dreams – often with orgasm – are common in both sexes. Maybe frustration again plays some part, since sexual energy is high in adolescence while opportunity may be restricted. But so does nature herself, who appears intent on trying out the mechanisms she has just brought to full development. In adult life, erotic dreams are frequent during the early stages of sexual abstinence (as for example in those who enter monasteries), but tend to tail off after two years or so, as if nature gets the message that that particular bodily function is no longer required by its owner.

Throughout life, erections in the male are common during dreaming, even when the dream itself has no overt sexual content. This is sometimes claimed to be due to the pressure of a full bladder upon the nerves concerned, but a more likely explanation is that the neurological relaxation of NREM sleep followed by the greater neurological activity of dreaming sleep stimulates the blood-flow into the penis and produces erection. Since nature usually has a reason for her activities, this may be her way of keeping the mechanism in good working order. And few men would quarrel with that.

You can use dreams to solve problems. Dreams themselves, as I pointed out in the Introduction, are highly creative experiences, and since problem-solving often demands a creative approach it's logical that if we can bring at least some aspects of our dreaming under conscious control, we may be able to use it to help us with our waking problems.

The evidence that we can indeed do so is strong, as we shall see in Chapter 3. (On a related subject, the evidence that we can *learn* during sleep by playing a tape to ourselves isn't strong at all, more's the pity.)

You don't carry your moral code into your dreams. It was Freud who was primarily responsible for this one (see Chapter 2). In Freudian theory our moral sense, together with the rest of our conscious mind, nods off during sleep, leaving the unconscious mind, with all its amoral instinctive urges, to take over. The area awaits more research, but my own dreams show I'm perfectly capable of taking moral decisions consistent with my waking conscience while I'm asleep, and I've no reason to believe I'm unique in this.

Conclusion

The extent of these conceptions and misconceptions about dreaming (and the above list isn't exhaustive) is further evidence of the extent to which dreams intrigue us. They are part of our lives and yet not part of our lives. They represent the world and ourselves in a way so different from our waking experiences that it seems almost as if we live in two separate worlds, the world of waking life and the world of dreams. In the end, of course, remember that you are the best authority on this latter world. You are the person who nightly enters it. Many of the questions you ask about it are best answered by you yourself. You are your own dream explorer, your own dream researcher. Never believe it otherwise.

2

DREAM INTERPRETATION ANCIENT AND MODERN

In ancient times, men and women took their understanding of life from direct experience. They accepted events at their face value. The sun rose in one horizon and set in the other, therefore the sun went round the earth. The stars made patterns in the heavens, therefore there must be a meaning to the stars. Dream events followed a different set of rules from waking life, therefore dreams were experiences of another kind of existence. No 'proof' was needed for this beyond the dream itself. Dreams were what they seemed to be.

And since information was conveyed in dreams which appeared to be outside the waking experience of the dreamer, it followed that wise beings – gods perhaps – spoke to you in dreams. If the information conveyed was unpleasant, it followed that malign influences could also make use of dreams. The enigmatic content of dreams was early recognised – whoever it was that spoke to you in dreams spoke in riddles, and left you to interpret their meaning for yourself. At the beginning of the present century Sigmund Freud, in one of the classic works on dreaming (*The Interpretation of Dreams*), identified two basic methods used by the ancients in this interpretation. The first took the dream as a whole and looked for an actual event which it might represent (for example Joseph's Old Testament interpretation of the dreams about seven fat and seven lean kine was taken to indicate seven fertile and seven famine years). The second took each dream image as a separate sign, and looked for its individual – often symbolic – meaning.

The Methods of the Early Egyptians

As early as 2,000 BC the Egyptians were using both these methods, and produced (in the so-called Chester Beatty papyrus) guidelines for applying them, the influence of many of which is still seen in the so-called Dream Dictionaries on sale today.

For example it was suggested that the whole dream could be interpreted in terms of opposites or contraries. An unhappy dream could therefore presage happiness, while a happy one could indicate the opposite. Individual images could be interpreted through association. If you dreamt, for example, of a shoe, and this suggested to your waking mind a boat and a journey over water, then just such a journey was either advisable or in fact lay ahead. Another possibility for individual interpretation was to use word similarities. If the word for the object of which you'd dreamt sounded like the word for another object, then the dream was really about this second object, no matter how remote it seemed from the first. (An example from modern English would be to interpret a dream about a mouse as conveying a message about your house.)

Not content simply with interpreting dreams, the Egyptians also developed ways for trying to induce them. In the best known of these, the would-be dreamer took a special potion of herbs and slept in the temple. The following morning he or she recounted the night's dream to the priest, who then interpreted its meaning. Under the influence of the Egyptians, the Babylonians and the Jews developed similar systems, but the Jews also took account of the personality, the background, the economic circumstances and so on of the dreamer. Thus although dreams were seen to carry common themes and symbols, these were recognised as subject to modification in individual cases.

The Ancient Greeks and After

The ancient Greeks borrowed extensively from both the Egyptian and the Babylonian systems, but not surprisingly saw dreams as coming from their own rather than from Egyptian or

Babylonian gods. They also borrowed the Egyptian method for inducing dreams, and over the years a number of shrines were established, many of them associated with the healing of physical illness. The most important of these were the ones dedicated to Aesculapius of Epidaurus, whose symbol was the snake (hence the snake symbol still used in modern Western medicine). The practice was for the subject to take his potion-induced sleep and the following morning have his dream scrutinised by the priest as a guide to diagnosis and healing. If he was particularly fortunate, he might even be cured by the dream itself, particularly if the god Aesculapius actually appeared in the course of it.

By the fifth century BC, however, Hippocrates began to change the way in which the Greeks thought about dreams, arguing that although they could be used in the diagnosis and treatment of disease this was because they reflected bodily states rather than because they were messages from the gods. In the third century BC Aristotle further advanced this thinking, arguing that if dreams really were messages from the gods they would only be sent to wise people who could make proper use of them. His conclusion was that dreams were essentially sparked off by the senses. Thus if one became too hot while asleep one would have a dream about fire and so on. Due to the link between the senses and dreams, he agreed with Hippocrates that they could also serve as early indications of physical illness of one sort or another.

The next important development occurred in the second century AD when the Roman Sophist Artemidorus (who makes a brief appearance in Shakespeare's *Julius Caesar*) proposed that dreams are in fact often a continuation of waking activities. Agreeing with the Jewish idea that dream interpretation must take into account the life circumstances of the dreamer, he produced no fewer than five books setting out guidelines for this interpretation.

The Early Christian Church

These five books influenced most systems of dream inter-pretation right up until the time of Freud. And although the trend away from the divine interpretation of dreams was partially reversed in the first centuries of Christianity (St John Chrysostum, St Augustine and St Jerome in the fourth century AD for example all taught that God reveals Himself in dreams), by medieval times the Church was firmly against the divine view. God's revelation was in and through the Church itself, and man had no need of dreams or of any other kind of direct access to Him. Thomas Aquinas' advice was to ignore dreams as much as possible, while Martin Luther's was that at most they simply showed us our sins.

Dreams were too strongly rooted in the popular imagination, however, to be dismissed thus easily, and with the growing availability of printed books from the fifteenth century onwards popular dream dictionaries – most of them based upon the systems of Artemidorus – began to proliferate. For all their naivety, these dream dictionaries fulfilled a useful function in that they took dream interpretation away from the priests and the seers who had traditionally controlled it, and suggested for the first time that each man or woman could be their own interpreter.

Although the importance of dreams was summarily rejected by the burgeoning scientific rationalism of the eighteenth century, which looked upon dream interpretation as just another form of superstition, few writers and poets were prepared to share this view, and dreams began to figure prominently in respectable eighteenth and nineteenth century literature. So much so that philosophers such as Fichte and Herbart began to take dreams seriously, and so see them as providing clues to the unconscious mind, theories about which were beginning to emerge from a number of quarters.

Dreams and the Unconscious

It was this link between dreams and the unconscious that was primarily responsible for the beginning of what we might call the scientific investigation of dreams. That is, an investigation which tried systematically to link dreams to underlying psychological and physiological causes, and to discover their significance, if any, for our psychological lives.

BOX 3
THE UNCONSCIOUS

The unconscious (sometimes wrongly called the subconscious) mind figures prominently in any discussion of dreams. In sleep, the conscious mind goes off duty, and the unconscious takes over and plays out our dreams for us. But what exactly *is* the unconscious? Psychologists talk of:

* the *conscious mind* – the things that are going through your head now

* the *pre-conscious* – the information stored in your head that you can recall at will

* and the *unconscious* – forgotten and repressed material, instinctive drives, all those things stored away somewhere inside us which influence our behaviour but which we can't access at will and which often (apart from what happens in dreams) can only be brought up into our consciousness with the aid of special techniques.

Using labels like 'conscious', 'pre-conscious' and 'unconscious' makes it sound as if these things have tangible separate existences, much like physical organs. But in fact these labels are simply convenient terms that psychologists use to help us discuss the mysterious workings of the mind.

Accessing the unconscious. One technique for getting in touch with your unconscious is hypnosis. Another is meditation (page 129). But a simple technique for you to try now is *free association*. In free association you can start with any word (an emotional or symbolic one is best) and allow it to set off a chain of associations in your mind which can lead to the sudden recall of long-forgotten memories or the upsurge of repressed emotion.
    Start with the word *water*. Hold it in your mind. What word or idea or image comes up in association with it? Hold that in your mind and see what comes up next. Now what comes up in association with that word or image? Go on from there, allowing each association to spark off the next, no matter how far these associations lead you away from the original word 'water'. Try the same exercise using other words as your starting point. Try *love*, or *circle* or *me* or *power* or *man* or *woman* or any other word that has great potential meaning. Don't be alarmed or frightened by what comes up. If negative or uncomfortable or even violent images surface, this doesn't mean that you are predominantly 'bad'. Everyone experiences these from time to time. They simply show that we have

---

BOX 3
THE UNCONSCIOUS

emotions or instincts or painful memories which we have
never been allowed to bring to the surface and lay to rest.

Now back to dreaming. By accessing your unconscious in this
way in your waking life, you also bring yourself more in
contact with your dream world. Sometimes dream memories
surface in the course of free association. And dreams
themselves become clearer, easier to remember, more
meaningful. Something of the distance between conscious
and unconscious begins to disappear.

Gone was any attempt to link dreams to the word of God, or
to use them for divining the future or in the diagnosis and
treatment of physical illness. In their place was the growing
conviction that dreams, along with all other psychological
phenomena, are *caused* in some way by physical processes, and
that careful observation would eventually reveal the exact
nature of this cause.

It was against this background that in late 1899 Freud's
monumental *The Interpretation of Dreams* made its appearance.

Freud and the Interpretation of Dreams

Though he summarised the work on dreams that had been
carried out over the centuries, Freud believed that virtually
alone and unaided he had actually solved, once and for all, the
mystery surrounding dreaming. 'Insight such as this,' he wrote
in the preface to the third English edition of the book, 'falls to
one's lot but once in a lifetime.' And as if the reading public
agreed, *The Interpretation of Dreams*, although it sold only 351
copies in the first six years after publication, eventually ran
through eight editions in the next 30 years, and must be listed
as one of the very few books that has changed Western man's
way of looking at himself.

For *The Interpretation of Dreams* did two things. Firstly it
established in the minds of many people that dreams deserve
scientific study and analysis. And secondly (as is true of Freud's

work as a whole), without necessarily providing the right answers it made clear the kind of questions we should ask during this study and analysis.

Essentially these questions are:

* What is the cause and the purpose of dreams?

* How should we interpret their meaning?

* How should we use this interpretation to understand more about the psychological life of the dreamer?

* How can this understanding help us in diagnosing and treating psychological problems?

* How can further dreams be used to monitor the progress of this treatment?

For like Hippocrates, Freud believed that dreams do give clues to our state of health, although in his case it was primarily *psychological* health that was involved, and not physical health.

In answering his own questions, Freud came to the conclusion that dreams are essentially *wish fulfilment*. In his theory of human psychology, he considered we are each born with strong instinctive drives which operate initially at an unconscious level, and which govern our emotional responses and provide us with our fundamental motivation in life. Chief amongst these drives, and from which even our nobler forms of behaviour arise through sublimation, are the ones for personal survival (the *self-preservation drive*) and for the survival of the species (the *sex drive*). The former manifests itself in such things as self-assertion and anger and aggression, and the latter in sexual arousal and intercourse. Although not 'bad' in themselves, problems arise in human psychology when the emotional energy associated with these instincts becomes excessively frustrated or punished.

This happens particularly in childhood, where the child is taught to conform to the rules and regulations of the adult world, with the result that he has to control and repress many of the things that his instincts strongly motivate him to do. Self-assertion, for example, is typically discouraged in the child, as is any expression of sexuality. The result is that the emotional energy behind these drives, instead of being acknowledged and consciously channelled into socially acceptable forms, becomes repressed and disowned. The child feels guilty about its very existence, and is never able to integrate it fully into his personality.

However, repressed energy does not simply go away. It persists at an unconscious level, from where it seeks an outlet when the controlling conscious mind is off its guard. Thus in sleep, when the conscious mind relinquishes its control, the repressed energy seeks expression and gratification in the form of dreams; in other words it fulfils those wishes which have not been allowed expression at a conscious level. Our repressed resentment or hostility towards others, for example, and our repressed sexual desires, act themselves out in the theatre of sleep, allowing the repressed energy a necessary form of release.

But although it relinquishes control, the conscious mind still remains alert enough to wake up in the face of what it perceives as threat of some kind, whether from the outside world or from disturbing experiences in our own dreams. Should the dream act out its fantasies in too blatant a manner, the conscious mind sees this as a threat to its moral sense, and accordingly wakes up (as can happen, for example, in nightmares or in sexual dreams). Therefore in order to allow us to stay asleep and continue dreaming, the unconscious expresses these fantasies in a largely disguised, symbolic form – hence the strange and often apparently meaningless character of our dreams.

In Freud's view this symbolic form shows remarkable consistency across cultures and between individuals, so much so that he considered it forms a universal symbolic language. A language which crops up not only in dreams but in such other deep outpourings of the unconscious as the great myths and legends of mankind. A language moreover which the psychotherapist can learn and, rather like the Egyptian priest, use in his or her interpretation of the client's dreams and the psychological states that underlie them.

For Freud, dreams thus have both a *manifest content* (what they seem to be) and a *latent content* (what they really are). If we are to use dreams to help understand the unconscious processes which in Freudian theory are seen to underlie most psychological disorders, we must therefore unravel the latent content of the dream, the hidden meaning that lies behind the manifest content. Dreams are, Freud argued, 'the royal road to the unconscious'. By unravelling their latent meaning we are able to bring to the surface the unconscious material that is causing our psychological disorders, and start the process of owning it and coming to proper terms with it.

To help in this unravelling, Freud developed the technique we used on page 34, namely *free association*. Through his clinical experience, he discovered that the technique was particularly effective with patients if he took as the starting point the images or ideas that occurred spontaneously in their dreams. And this procedure then became one of the cornerstones of psychoanalysis, the therapeutic technique developed by Freud and still one of the most widely used methods for working with neurotic problems.

Freud's theory of dreams reflected his belief in the vital role played in the development of our personalities by the self-preservation and the sexual instincts respectively. Which brings me to a vital caution in any approach to dream understanding and dream analysis. Namely that it is all too easy to read into dreams one's own particular theoretical persuasion as to the nature of mind and of human personality. Due to their extraordinary variety and richness, one can all too readily see in dreams what one wants to see, and Freud, like many other dream interpreters, was not immune to this weakness.

As I shall stress several times throughout the book, dreams can be understood on a number of different levels. To offer one single explanation of dreams and of dream interpretation is as unrealistic as to offer a single explanation for the varied richness of waking experience. But Freud performed an invaluable service in drawing attention to the psychological importance of dreaming, and from Freud onwards no *psychodynamic* psychologist (that is, no psychologist concerned with unconscious processes and with the view that human psychology is driven by deep emotional forces) has neglected dreaming.

The Work of Carl Jung

Of all such psychologists, Carl Jung is perhaps the outstanding example. Jung's theories on dreams differed from those of Freud in that he saw the unconscious as the seat not only of the self-preservation and sexual drives identified by Freud, but also of higher motivational drives such as creativity and spirituality. Thus dreams are not simply wish fulfilments of our repressed desires, but also the language in which our higher, wiser self can speak to us. In dreams we find the key not only to what is causing our present problems, but also to what we most need to do to put them right and to develop our full potential as human beings. Dreams are thus primarily a compensatory mechanism. They compensate for the errors and omissions in our conscious understanding.

Jung described each of us as living in a splendid house, yet seldom moving out of the basement. That is, we are full of potentialities – for experience, for achievement, for creative expression, for psychological and spiritual growth – which we not only fail to explore but of whose very existence we often live and die in complete ignorance. In dreams we find a means of discovering some of the other rooms in our house. In dreams we leave the basement and wander the vast corridors and staircases of our mind, sometimes discovering secret, unpleasant dark rooms which fill us with fear and anxiety, sometimes finding rooms full of useless lumber, but sometimes opening doors to rooms filled with sunlight and beauty, whose windows look out onto sweeping magical landscapes criss-crossed with roads and pathways leading towards the sunrise and the distant hills.

Just as we find many rooms in our house, so we meet many people. Some of them familiar, some of them strange and unknown. Some of them friendly, some of them apparently menacing and hostile. All of them have something to teach us. As we begin to read and understand our dream symbols so we become able to listen to this teaching. For Jung as for Freud, the dream is deeply symbolic, containing both a manifest and a latent meaning. Dreams should not be taken at their face value. Few things in dreams are what they seem. If they were, we would risk being overwhelmed by what they have to tell us. Dreams reveal their secret messages to us in proportion to the ability of our conscious mind to understand and cope with them. Dream interpretation is a slow process, fraught with error and misunderstanding, but this in a sense is for our own protection. If we were confronted too abruptly with our hidden self, the conscious mind could well be swept away by it.

Like Freud, Jung encouraged his clients to provide free associations to the ideas and images in dreams in order to unlock their symbolic meaning. But unlike Freud, he did not encourage his clients to wander too far during free association from the dream itself. His advice was always to keep coming back to the dream symbol, and start each time from that. Losing sight of the symbol risked losing sight of the dream's real meaning, and becoming lost in free associations which in the end might have little to do with this meaning. The symbol itself held the key, and the mind must not be allowed to sidetrack into involved free associations and thus avoid confronting the deep issues which the symbol represented.

Like Freud however, Jung took a deep interest in the great myths and legends of mankind, and in the symbols used in the world's religions (such as the cross, the circle, the star, the eagle, the lion). Through an understanding of these out-pourings of the creative human imagination, we can learn the language of dreams. Each man and woman is free to invent his or her own symbols (usually at an unconscious level), but the symbols we each of us invent usually show a remarkable similarity. For Jung, this was because we inherit not only our physical and mental characteristics, but also a *collective unconscious*, that is, an innate tendency to organise and interpret our experience in similar ways to each other.

The content of the collective unconscious is expressed primarily in symbols, or as Jung called them *archetypes*. Archetypes are thus primeval images and ideas, meaningful for all races and at all times, and found not only in myths and legends but also in children's fairy stories and in artistic expression. We each of us can modify and personify these archetypes in our own way (for Jung symbols were not 'fixed' as they could be for Freud), but easily recognisable examples are the wise old man, the witch, the trickster (who constantly challenges us and upsets our plans and our complacency), the hero, the beautiful woman, the magician and the wise animal in one form or another. Many of our dream symbols are only understandable in terms of their archetypal meaning, and a study of the archetypes is desirable for anyone interested in Jungian dream interpretation.

A comparison between Freud and Jung provides us with examples of the different levels of dreaming that I mentioned earlier. Some dreams operate at what I term the *mundane symbolic level*, namely the level of Freud's self-preservation drives and sex drives, while others operate at what I term the *elevated symbolic level*, that is Jung's higher order level of psychological and spiritual understanding and growth. In dream interpretation, we have to be alert to these two levels, and allow the dreamer him or herself ultimately to identify on which level a particular dream is operating. Let's make this comparison between Freud and Jung (Box 4) then summarise these two symbolic levels.

BOX 4
FREUDIAN AND JUNGIAN DREAM INTERPRETATIONS

It's revealing to look at examples of Freudian and Jungian interpretations respectively. I'll use two dreams which contain an identifical theme, namely the death of the dreamer's mother. Firstly an example from Freud.

A young woman in therapy with Freud had the feeling that she didn't want to see any of her relatives again, as they 'must think me horrible'. She then recalled a dream she had had when four years old of a lynx walking on the roof of her house, then of herself or something else falling down, then of her mother 'being carried dead out of the house'.

In the analysis of the dream, Freud concluded it meant that as a child she had wished to see her mother dead, and that it was because of this repressed wish she now felt all her relatives hated her. In further support of this interpretation, the young woman remembered that as a very young child she had been called 'lynx-eyed' as a term of abuse by another child, and that when she was three years old a tile had fallen off the roof, hitting her mother and making her head bleed profusely.

Now an example from Jung. Again the dreamer is a young woman. In her dream she comes home late at night to find the house 'as quiet as death'. In the living room she sees her mother hanged from the chandelier, her body 'swinging to and fro' in the cold wind from the open window. In the dream analysis, Jung concludes that 'mother' is being used by the dreaming mind as an archetypal symbol for the unconscious, and that the dream is therefore telling the dreamer that her

---

BOX 4

FREUDIAN AND JUNGIAN DREAM INTERPRETATIONS

'unconscious life is destroying itself'. He also correctly predicted that it gave warning of grave physical illness.

These two examples don't indicate a necessary conflict between Freud and Jung over the meaning of the dream image 'mother'. Rather they show that in dream interpretation we must study this and all other images in context. In the case of Freud's patient, the association of 'lynx' with a term of abuse, plus the actual memory of a tile falling on the mother's head and causing injury, were sufficient to confirm Freud in his belief that the actual parent was the subject of the dream, and that the dream acted out the patient's repressed hostility towards her.

In the case of Jung's patient, there was no evidence of this kind, and the analysis thus looked for deeper meaning.

These two examples are presented here in very shortened form. In both cases the interpretation concerned would have involved much more detail than I have been able to give, and would have been set against the many other insights into the patients' lives that had emerged in the course of therapist-patient interaction. But they show something of the complexity of dream interpretation, and of the vital importance of studying each dream on an individual basis rather than taking over interpretations ready made from dream dictionaries.

The Two Symbolic Levels

Mundane symbolic level. Concrete and physical, and related on the one hand to basic self-preservation needs such as nutrition, bodily comfort and health, physical exercise, physical gratification and personal power; and to self-preservation emotions such as anger, fear, and the need to seek sympathy, nurturing and support from others.

And related on the other hand to sexual needs such as erotic sensations, sensuality, and sexual dominance or submission.

Higher symbolic level. More mental and abstract, and related to our urge to find meaning in life beyond self-preservation and sex. The motivation behind much creative activity, behind altruism and selflessness, and behind mystical and spiritual experiences.

Other Dreamworkers

Both Freud and Jung are so important to our story that they will crop up again in the pages that follow. But is the belief, so central to their theory and practice, that dreams use a complex symbolic language accepted by all other psychologists involved in dreamwork? The answer is that they are accepted by many (particularly by those whose approach is psychodynamic) but not by all. Space allows us only two examples of psychologists who take a markedly different approach, but the ideas of both of them have proved highly influential. The first accepts the symbolism of dreams but in a much more simplified form, while the second rejects symbolism altogether.

The first of these psychologists is Fritz Perls, the founder of gestalt therapy. For Perls, dream interpretation must start from the point that all characters and objects in the dream are in fact symbols, projections of ourselves and of the way we have been living our lives. Thus they are often parts of our personality which may currently be unacknowledged by our waking, conscious mind. The logic of this is that since we are each the authors of our own dreams, whatever we put into them must first of all be within us. Perls therefore differed from Freud and Jung in arguing firstly that dream symbolism is the personal creation of each of us rather than part of a universal symbolic language, and secondly that it should be seen as connected with our life experiences to date rather than with innate instinctive drives.

In Perls' view, dreams for the most part represent unfinished emotional business carried over from these life experiences ('emotional holes' as Perls called them), and the therapeutic use of dreams therefore consists of getting at the personal emotional nuances that lie behind the dream imagery. To do this, Perls developed his *role-play* exercises, where the dreamer is called upon to speak out in turn for each of the significant characters or objects in his or her dream. Thus in, for example, a dream of travelling by train, one should speak out not just in the role of the guard or the driver or of fellow passengers but also of the railway carriage and the railway track (and find perhaps that the latter is a part of the personality fiercely resentful of always being underneath, always being taken for granted, always being ridden over by the wheels, the engine, the carriages, the passengers – in fact by other aspects of the personality and of one's life experience).

This approach shows another important break from Freudian or Jungian dream interpretations in that the dreamer does his or her own interpretation, in terms of his or her own symbolic language. The therapist may of course make suggestions, and if the work is being carried out in a group (another of Perl's departures from conventional dream work) other members of the group can also make contributions. But essentially the dream is the property of the dreamer, and he or she must never have meaning imposed upon it from outside.

The second example of a psychologist who rejected Freudian and Jungian dream symbolism is Medard Boss, who was among the founders of existential psychology, a psychology based upon the belief that each of us chooses what we wish to be and expresses our choice in every aspect of our behaviour. Boss broke with the centuries-old tradition that dreams always carry a manifest and a latent content, and developed instead a method which allowed the dream to tell its own story. All that is needed in this method, Boss claimed, is a mind uncluttered by theoretical preconceptions and by a knowledge of esoteric symbolism.

The dream interpreter should therefore have the ability, apparently simple but in reality hard to come by, of seeing clearly and accurately what is there before his or her eyes. Using this clarity and accuracy, Boss argued, most dreams reveal very quickly the dreamer's existential condition, bringing it home to him or her, often with shattering impact.

An example of the way in which Boss demonstrated his theory was to hypnotise five women – three healthy and two neurotic – and to suggest to them they should each dream about a man known to be in love with them, experiencing him naked, sexually aroused, and advancing towards them with clear sexual intent.

It is certainly possible to use the hypnotic state to influence a person's dream content, and Boss's women dutifully dreamt of their respective male friends. The three healthy women enjoyed the dream enormously (some might say with good reason),

BOX 5
DREAM INTERPRETATIONS BY PERLS AND BOSS

Perls' method of dream interpretation involved a great deal of verbal interaction between himself (together with members of the dream workshop) and the person recounting a dream, together with much acting out of the various elements in the dream. Attention was also paid to the latter's physical posture, since this reflected something of the emotions he or she had felt while dreaming, together with elements of his or her present emotional state. So it isn't easy to give a proper account of a Perls' dream workshop in a short space. But the following example gives something of the flavour.

The dream is of a lake drying up; the dreamer is concerned about this, but consoles herself with the thought that there will be treasure on the lake bed. But when the water has disappeared all she discovers is an old licence plate. Asked by Perls to play the role of the licence plate she comes up with 'I am no use because I'm no value… outdated… I don't like being a licence plate… the use of a licence plate is to give a car permission to go… I can't give anyone permission to do anything because I'm outdated.' Asked to play the lake she says 'I'm drying up… disappearing… soaking into the earth… so maybe I water the surrounding area… new life… can grow from me.' The interpretation that emerges is that nature doesn't need a licence plate (an artificial artefact) to grow – the dreamer doesn't have to be useless or to need permission to be creative, provided she allows herself to be involved in life.

Now here is an example of an analysis by Boss. The dream is of being far above the earth and seeing a nuclear war about to break out between the great powers. No living people represent these great powers, only blocks of stone or chess pieces. A nuclear bomb falls into the sea, and the dreamer knows that something, pehaps a big fish down in the depths, has the power to explode it.

Discussing his dream, the dreamer wonders if the earth symbolises his personality, and the great powers his own embattled mental abilities. Boss rejects this. The dream means what it says. The dreamer's relationship to the world and everything in it is a distant one. He has reduced people to the status of inanimate objects or of chessmen. He is worried about the possibility of world catastrophe, but does nothing about it, remaining a passive observer. The one living element in the dream world (the fish) is hidden and is just as threatening as the blocks of stone and the chessmen.

BOX 5
DREAM INTERPRETATIONS BY PERLS AND BOSS

The dream shows clearly that the dreamer is a self-isolated, frightened man who has lost his footing in the world. There is nothing to be gained by trying to read any other kind of meaning into it.

The issues raised by these interpretations are returned to in Chapter 5.

---

dreaming of the scenario exactly as suggested by Boss and relating it to him with considerable gusto. The two neurotic women however missed the fun, and produced very anxious and unarousing versions. In one case the dream was not overtly of the lover at all but of a uniformed soldier advancing with a handgun, in the course of playing with which he nearly shot her, frightening her into awaking.

If we examine these dreams we see that in the case of the three healthy women the dreams had no obviously disguised content. They were certainly wish-fulfilments, but far from being of repressed unacknowledged material, they openly reflected the dreamer's conscious desires. 'Ah!' a Freudian would argue, 'but perhaps the dreamer simply *used* the naked lover as a symbol for some much deeper material. Maybe he stood for her desire to have intercourse with some other male. Perhaps he symbolized her incestuous love for her father. Perhaps he symbolised something to do with power and dominance. And what about the dreams of the two neurotic women? Surely the handgun was a symbol for her unacknowledged feelings towards her lover's penis, while being nearly shot by it symbolised ejaculation or indeed even attempted intercourse?'

Boss would answer that in the case of the healthy women we need look no further than the dream at its face value. Nothing is gained by trying to read symbolism into it. And even in the case of the neurotic dream about a gun, surely the correct procedure is simply to see it as revealing the narrow, fear-drenched world of the dreamer. Such a world has no place for a sexually aroused and arousing lover. Within it, men are seen as intrusive and dangerous, and as uniform and faceless in their menace. Nothing is to be gained by seeing the gun as symbolising a penis instead of simply as itself, an object of her fear and revulsion. In fact, in both the healthy and the neurotic dreams, any attempt at symbolic interpretation is actually counter-productive, since it detracts from the emotional impact of the dreams themselves. And the emotional impact is what carries much of the dream message.

Symbolic Versus Non-Symbolic Dream Interpretation

The symbolic and the non-symbolic approaches are not necessarily as contradictory as at first sight appears. Both have their uses. We must be a little careful about how much we read into the results of Boss's work with his five women subjects, since their dreams sprang from his hypnotic suggestions rather than from their own unconsciousness. But assuming the women reported the dreams correctly (the hypnotised mind is notoriously inclined to create fantasies which afterwards are taken for realities) the results certainly show that people can dream about things purely at face value.

Or that they can dream about them at face value *at one level*. For let me emphasise here the vital point, overlooked by many psychologists but which we must understand if we are success-fully to work with dreams, namely that like many of the events of waking life, dreams *can carry multiple meaning*. In the case of Boss's three psychologically healthy women, the dream events may therefore indeed have disguised other, deeper levels of meaning.

So the Freudian argument that the aroused lover could have symbolised some aspect of the subject's unconscious mind can certainly have truth in it. For example, as in Perls' approach, he could have symbolised the perhaps unrecognised masculine side of the subject's own nature. And in the case of the two neurotic women, something could in fact be gained by exploring whether the gun served in the dream as a symbol of the penis. For it might be that the subject was not frightened of all aspects of masculinity but only of male sexuality, and it would be impor-tant to know this. Equally importantly, something could be gained by exploring the image of the soldier 'playing' with his own gun and causing it to go off. There are possible symbols

here for auto-eroticism, and the fact that the dreamer was
nearly shot as a result of this 'play' may indicate a deep-seated
fear and guilt of such eroticism in herself.

These are speculations. But only a more open form of dream
interpretation, which worked with the subject and her dream at
both face and symbolic levels, could tease out whether these
deeper levels were operating or not. Certainly dreams *can* work
symbolically, and I present plenty of evidence to show this
throughout the book. By concentrating only at face value,
important symbolic meanings may therefore be overlooked.
But this doesn't mean that dreams cannot carry a straightforward meaning too, and we must take care that in our search
for symbols we don't overlook this level of interpretation either.

The presence of this straightforward meaning indicates we
have to add another level to the two already identified, and I call
this the *non-symbolic* or *face-value* level. It's convenient to number
the levels as follows, though this numbering doesn't necessarily
represent the existence of a rigid herarchy between them:

Level One: Non-Symbolic Level
Level Two: Mundane Symbolic Level
Level Three: Higher Symbolic Level

At Which Level Should We Work in Dream Interpretation?

We may never be able fully to unravel the mystery of dreams,
since there are no – and may never be – precise instruments
available for exploring the deeper levels of the human mind. In
their absence, we have to be guided by what is helpful. If a
particular level of interpretation helps people towards a fuller
understanding and a more effective reshaping of their lives,
then in an acceptable sense that interpretation is 'true'. This is
not as imprecise an approach as it may seem. Even in the most
rigorously orthodox scientific theories, the acid test is still one of
usefulness. It was Jung who, in psychology and in life generally,
equated usefulness with truth. And since no scientific theory
can be anything more than a man-made model of reality, to be
'believed' until it is superseded by something more useful still,
the equation of dream truth with usefulness isn't badly out of
step with what happens in other areas of human thinking.

I shall have much more to say about these three different levels of interpretation when I discuss detailed ways of working with your own dreams in Chapter 5.

Other Cultures, Other Approaches

So in the four psychological approaches we have just examined, we have four different kinds of usefulness. Freud with his emphasis upon our instinctive drives and upon the dream as a wish fulfilment for our frustrated wishes in waking life (Level Two). Jung with his recognition of man's higher self, and emphasis upon the dream as compensation and as a gateway to wisdom (Level Three). Perls with his focus upon the dream as representing aspects of ourselves and our life experiences (Levels Two and Three), and Boss with his stress upon the dream as a face value guide to our present condition and to what existential psychologists call our 'being-in-the-world' (Level One).

But before we leave this examination of different approaches to dream work, something must be said about the approaches of other, non-Western cultures. I spoke in the Introduction about the hold dreaming has across races as well as across the centuries, and it is interesting to look at what two of the most important of these approaches, the American Indian and the Senoi, have to tell us.

For the American Indian, dreams were a way of telling the future, of managing psychological problems, and – most importantly of all – of contacting supernatural beings and obtaining power from them. Different tribes had different methods for inducing, interpreting and using dreams, but fairly common to them all was a strong belief in motivation, in the strength of will of the dreamer. If you wished for a particular kind of dream, offering you particular kinds of help and guidance, and concentrated upon it for a sufficient period of time, then it would eventually be given to you. Fasting, prayer, meditation and retreating to an isolated spot were all helpful. Sometimes in the dream the dreamer would meet a spirit helper, who would remain with him, reappearing regularly in dreams, for as long as was needed. Sometimes the dreamer would learn a song in a dream, or a special skill, such as understanding the ways of animals.

Sometimes, particularly if one aspired to becoming a shaman (a medicine man) one would wander among the spirits of the dead and learn secrets from them. Or one would take part in single-handed combat, or be torn apart by savage creatures and undergo a ritual death, only to be reassembled and reborn into a new personality, wiser and more powerful than the old one. The dream would serve as an initiation into new ways of being, a transformation into a new and more extensive and magical reality.

For the Senoi people in the mountain jungles of Malaysia, dreams provide a somewhat similar function, although the emphasis is more upon transforming the dream experience in positive and pleasurable directions while it is actually taking place. Although not described in such terms by the Senoi, their dreamwork is directed towards emotional health. If you are menaced by danger in dreams, turn and confront it. If you are offered pleasure, go towards it. If someone tries to teach you something, listen to them. Working on one's dream emotions in this way is thought to help one's emotions in waking life. Instead of one-way traffic, with the emotional experiences of our waking lives affecting the emotional content of dreams, traffic can flow the other way too, and the emotional content of dreams can affect the emotional experiences of our waking lives. Learning fearlessness in dreams thus helps us to be fearless in waking life, spontaneous acceptance of pleasure helps us to be spontaneous, listening to wisdom helps us to be wise.

This belief sounds strange to many Western psychologists, but there's no real reason why it should. We know that dream emotions can influence our waking feelings. A bad dream can leave us upset for days, a good dream can leave us filled with joy. Since dreams are so intimately connected with our emotions at deep and fundamental levels, there's no rational reason why the emotional lessons we learn in them shouldn't have a permanent effect upon the way we feel about and react to life.

Earlier anthropologists may have over-emphasised the part that dreams play in the life of the Senoi, offering us largely uncorroborated tales of children being asked each morning to recount their dreams over the family breakfast. But there's no doubt that both the American Indians and the Senoi show a clear belief in the possibility of gaining direct and beneficial *control* over dreams. Our knowledge that this skill is possible comes from other sources as well, and some of the later exercises in this book are designed to help you work on this skill in your own dreaming.

Finally, a word about dreaming in the great spiritual traditions of the East. In these traditions it is also taken for granted that you can work upon and gain control of your dream life, in this case primarily for the purposes of spiritual development. For example, it is claimed that the teacher can appear to the pupil in dream life (and vice versa), and that the following morning both will know that the visit has taken place and will agree on what has been said. More strikingly still, it is claimed that the dreamer can remain conscious throughout his or her dreaming, and that the height of achievement is when consciousness persists throughout sleep, flowing uninterruptedly through the waking hours, through dreaming sleep, and through dreamless sleep.

Advanced practitioners also teach that slipping from wakefulness into sleep is a dress rehearsal for death, a dress rehearsal through which we each of us go every night. If we can learn to make proper use of this dress rehearsal by keeping our consciousness continuous, this teaches us how to die. The same practitioners also teach the techniques which are said to make this possible, but these deserve a more extended discussion and will have to wait until Chapter 8.

3

CREATIVITY, INTELLIGENCE AND DREAMING

Creativity, like dreaming, relies heavily upon the unconscious. Notice how, in creative activity, you may work on an idea or a problem until you get stuck, then dismiss it from your conscious mind only to find that some time later (the following morning perhaps, or days, weeks, even years afterwards) the development of the idea or the solution to the problem pops into your mind ready-made. Many great writers and scientists over the centuries have reported this phenomenon. It seems that the unconscious mind goes on working on the problem even though consciously you have forgotten all about it. Psychologists call this process *incubation*. The unconscious tries one possible solution after another until suddenly it recognises it has hit upon something that might be helpful, and pushes it up into your conscious mind for you to have a look at. We can call it, if we like, the 'Eureka' phenomenon.

In my own writing, if I'm faced with a sentence or a paragraph that won't come out right, the best strategy is to get up from my desk, make myself a cup of tea or coffee or take a stroll around the garden thinking of anything but my literary endeavours. When I return to my desk a few minutes later, the sentence or paragraph usually comes to mind without further problem. It's surely the most painless way of arriving at a solution imaginable. My unconscious does the work for me, and very grateful I am to it.

In much the same way, our unconscious does the work for us in our dreams. It creates them without our conscious help. We are simply the fascinated (or reluctant) actors in a ready-made script. As in the creative act in waking life, the unconscious functions coherently and independently of our conscious thinking, bringing us adventures and ideas which carry the same shock of surprise as if they were written by a total stranger.

Creativity in waking life and creativity in dreams are alike also in that the representations of reality they produce can be equally realistic and vivid. Through his or her creative imagination (*imaging-action*; the creation of images) the creative artist can produce detailed landscapes, human and animal faces, a world as lifelike as the view from our own windows, or a world so strange and evocative it can open a new dimension in our experience. So too does the artist who illustrates our dreams. Even people who claim they are incapable of visualisation in waking life nevertheless see in their dreams a world so recognisable that it engages them as closely as does their daytime experience, and can linger as long in the mind to disturb and excite.

Another similarity is that in both creativity and dreams we often have little or no idea of the outcome. Novelists talk of the characters in their novels 'taking over' and deciding the rest of the plot for themselves. Painters (who perhaps more than any other artists use the language of the unconscious) talk of experimenting with shapes and colours until suddenly images leap into life. Musicians start with simple musical themes and end with major symphonies. Children build fantasy play-time worlds which dissolve and change like enchanted kingdoms. (At primary school I whiled away the lunchtimes telling my friends stories in which they were characters, and whose denouement I awaited with a curiosity no less than their own.)

Just so in dreams are we taken into the unknown. Our unconscious decides on the setting of the dream, on the characters, on the plot, on the ending. Or sometimes on the absence of an ending, for if it chooses it can stop the dream tantalisingly in mid-story, like a film breaking down, leaving our conscious mind ever afterwards to ponder on what might have been.

Yet another similarity is the way in which both creative experiences in waking life and experiences in dreams have the ability to engage us emotionally as deeply as the most moving of real life events. We cry over stories, and we awake crying over dreams. Stories terrify us, enrich us, amuse us, excite us, intrigue us. So it is with dreams. Poetry, music, paintings, sculpture stir our humanity into a recognition of the numinous and the divine. So it is with dreams. In defiance of all logic, these simulations of reality at times outdistance even reality itself, and may even call into question where reality really resides, in waking life or in dreams. As it did for example with the third century BC Chinese sage Chuang-Tzu, who tells us 'One night I dreamt I was a butterfly....Who am I in reality? A butterfly dreaming I am Chuang-Tzu or Chuang-Tzu imagining he was a butterfly?'

Finally, both creativity and dreams satisfy some deep urge that lies inside the human spirit. Man never leaves the world as he finds it. The urge to transform it, to reproduce it in other shapes and in other materials, seems innate in us. We see this urge in children's play, in many of our recreational (*re-creational*) activities, even in the doodles we make on scraps of paper during dull meetings. But we see it particularly in art, in science and in dreams. Our human spirit has a restlessness about it, a constant questing and seeking, a desire to search beyond the mundane and the familiar, to look into the distance and see what it can find. To take a piece of wood and turn it into a boat or a musical instrument or the image of a god. To invest the life around it with a life of its own making. Creative people are rarely happy unless they are creating. Even self-confessed uncreative people find many of their psychological problems vanish in the face of therapies which unlock their creative powers. Man, in a very real sense, is born to create, and without this creativity he cannot venture into those splendid upper rooms of his personality of which I spoke earlier.

So dreams are there in part to satisfy this creative urge. To provide it with heightened inspiration in creative people, to keep it from fading altogether in the less creative. To deny our creativity is to deny part of our life, and to deny our dreaming is to deny a tributary of the splendid river through which our creativity flows.

Creativity in Dreams

A valuable way of looking more closely at these links between creativity and dreaming, and of exploring how dreaming can enchance our own creativity, is to look at examples of dream creativity in famous people. One of the best known is the strange dream that inspired Coleridge's poem *Kubla Khan*. Coleridge was in poor health at the time, and after taking laudanum (a tincture of opium commonly prescribed in the eighteenth and nineteenth centuries) he dropped asleep while reading in a travel book the words 'Here the Kubla Khan commanded a palace to be built.' When he woke, the poem describing the building of Kubla Khan's pleasure dome was there, ready-made in his mind, and only needed to be written down. Unfortunately before he'd completed the task a visitor arrived on business (the shadowy 'person from Porlock', who makes only this one sad incursion into literary history). Coleridge went to attend to him, and when he returned to his study an hour later the rest of the poem, in the infuriating habit of dreams, had disappeared. Try as he might, Coleridge could not recapture it, and *Kubla Khan* was destined to remain an evocative and beautiful fragment rather than the literary masterpiece it might well have become.

As I mentioned on page 27, drugs tend to depress dreaming, so there is no reason simply to put Coleridge's dream down to the effects of opium. It is more relevant to put it down to the great interest he took in dreams. In one of the most intriguing questions posed by any poet, he ponders elsewhere what would happen if we dreamt of the gardens of Paradise, and plucked a flower, and found upon awaking the flower beside us on our pillow ('Ah what then?', he asks, 'what then?')

Robert Louis Stevenson was another writer who drew inspiration for his work from his dreams. In his memoirs he tells us that by working on his dreams – through the simple method of telling himself stories as he was going to sleep – he found that his 'little people' (as he called them) carried on the task for him during the night, setting forth tale after tale for him 'upon their lighted theatre'. One of Stevenson's most famous stories, *The Strange Case of Dr Jekyll and Mr Hyde*, was the result in part of this method, and Stevenson conceded generously that his little people deserved credit for the bulk of his writing.

Another example, but this time of a poet who actually received scientific inspiration in dreams, was William Blake. Blake illustrated his poems with his own engravings, but the technique was expensive, and he found himself 'intensely thinking by day and dreaming by night' of how to come by a cheaper alternative, but with no success. At last one night in a dream his dead brother Robert appeared to him and 'revealed the wished-for secret', namely a process of copper engraving. The next morning Blake sent his wife out with their last half crown to buy the simple materials 'necessary for setting in practice the new revelation', and Blake was launched upon the principal means of support for his future life. With Blake's mystical mind, he was convinced it really was his dead brother visiting him from the next world, and literature generally contains numerous other accounts of people who claim their dead loved ones have spoken to them in similar ways.

Hearing music in dreams and then making use of it in their own compositions is by no means uncommon amongst musicians. (Even as a relative non-musician I remember once waking from sleep with the most exquisite tune in my mind; regrettably it decided not to waste itself on me and I lost it the moment I became fully conscious.) One of the most celebrated examples is the eighteenth-century Italian composer Tartini, to whom the devil appeared in sleep and played on Tartini's own fiddle a sonata whose beauty Tartini tells us 'surpassed the wildest flights of my imagination'. Struggling unsuccessfully to recall it properly upon waking, Tartini nevertheless wrote the *Trillo del Diavola (The Devil's Trill)* which he considered the best thing he had ever done.

Among the very many other creative men and women who claim their work was inspired at times by their dreams are Sir Walter Scott, John Keats, Charlotte Brontë, Mark Twain, Edgar Alan Poe, H. G. Wells, Katherine Mansfield, Graham Greene, J. B. Priestley, and Jack Kerouac. One can only guess at how many others have kept quiet about the same source of inspiration for fear of not having their work taken seriously. (Or, more reprehensibly, for fear of losing personal credit for it.)

One can also only guess at the number of people who have received inspiration in dreams and been unable to recall it in the morning. The belief expressed by some people that inspiration of this kind, no matter how world-shaking it seems to be in the dream itself, always turns out to be trivial if it *is* recalled is shown to be untrue by the examples I've just given and also by the ones in the next section. And here's a personal example of a short poem I dreamt recently and wrote down immediately on waking.

> Come fly with me to Camden Town
> And I'll buy you a silken gown,
> Red roses for your shining hair,
> And velvet dreams beyond compare.

There may be those who say such an example only goes to support the argument that what seems world-shaking in dreams turns out to be trivial on waking, but my reply is that *I* enjoyed the poem as much on waking as in dreaming. And I was pleased that it did manage to stay in my memory long enough to be recorded for posterity (though whether posterity will be equally pleased about it is another matter).

What, I have to concede, *may* be a more telling example is that of the writer A. C. Benson, a prolific recorder of dreams. The reason for quoting it is that Benson claimed that the poem (which he wrote down in the middle of the night immediately on waking) came without conscious volition, was in a style that in waking life he never attempted before or since, and consisted of symbolism which he could neither understand nor interpret.

> By feathers green across Casbeen,
>   The pilgrims track the Phoenix flown,
> By gems he strewed in waste and wood
>   And jewelled plumes at random thrown.
>
> Till wandering far, by moon and star,
>   They stand beside the fruitful pyre,
> Whence breaking bright with sanguine light,
>   The impulsive bird forgets his sire.
>
> Those ashes shine like ruby wine,
>   Like bag of Tyrian murex spilt,
> The claw, the jowl of the flying fowl
>   Are with the glorious anguish gilt.

> So rare the light, so rich the sight,
>   Those pilgrim men, on profit bent,
> Drop hands and eyes and merchandise,
>   And are with gazing most content.

Problem Solving in Dreams

The artistic creativity exemplified in the last section is a form of problem solving. Deciding on the plot for a novel, or on the exact words to convey a particular emotion in a poem, or how best to use a particular theme in music or to realise a painting or a piece of sculpture are in their way just as much problems as is how to split the atom or how to get a quart into a pint pot.

But if creativity in its various forms is problem solving, so equally is intelligence. The difference between creativity and intelligence is primarily that the former operates in situations where the solution to our problems is a divergent, open-ended one, with many possibilities and with no final right or wrong answers. The latter operates, by contrast, in situations where the solution is a convergent, focused one which is either correct or incorrect. In many instances the two are called upon to work together, with creativity operating, so to speak, as the author, and intelligence as the editor. The author throws up a range of possible ideas, and the editor gets to work and decides which of them is most suitable for the purpose in hand. This is the case, for example, with certain scientific problems. There are many *apparently* possible ways to the solution, and the mind has to generate a range of them so that each in its turn can be put to the test until one is found that actually works.

In a sense, this is also the case with works of art. The creative mind spawns the ideas, which the intelligent mind then goes over, judges for suitability, and moulds into shape. But if, as we've just seen from the above examples, dreams can spawn ideas, can they also do the judging and moulding? Can dreams act both as authors and as editors? R. L. Stevenson tells us that after his 'little people' had done their work for him, his waking mind had to assess its value, sometimes finding it to be disappointing and unmarketable. For him at least, dreams might be the author but the waking mind had to be the editor.

Do Dreams Show Intelligence as Well as Creativity?

Put another way, Stevenson's dreams were creative, but not particularly intelligent. Is this because intelligence is the exclusive preserve of the conscious mind, and the unconscious processes of dreaming have nothing to do with it? Not really. Stevenson's dreams worked that way for him, but there are many instances of scientists solving very precise problems in dreams, or obtaining such clear clues to them that the conscious mind was left with very little work to do. One of the best known examples is that of the German chemist Friedrich Kekulé, who in 1890 claimed publicly to his colleagues that his discovery of the molecular structure of benzene a quarter of a century earlier came to him in a dream. (For those who see nothing very remarkable about discovering the molecular structure of benzene I should point out that it provided the key to modern molecular chemistry.)

The molecular structure of benzene is in the form of a chain of molecules arranged in the shape of a ring, and Kekulé describes his dreams as showing him

> ... the [molecules] gambolling before my eyes...frequently two smaller [ones] united to form a pair...a larger one embraced the smaller ones...still larger ones kept hold of three or four of the smaller, while the whole kept whirling in a giddy dance...My mental eye, rendered more acute by repeated visions of this kind, could now distinguish larger structures of manifold confirmation; long rows, sometimes more closely fitted together; all twining and twisting in snakelike motion. But look! What was that? One of the snakes had seized hold of its own tail, and the form whirled mockingly before my eyes. As if by a flash of lightning, I awoke.

Thus the benzene ring, as it is called, presented itself to Kekulé in the form of a snake seizing hold of its own tail. But for Kekulé this snake symbolism was so clear that he grasped its meaning at once. Thus for him the solution given in the dream was a convergent one, and provides unequivocal evidence that dreams can indeed behave intelligently.

But in that case, why use symbolism at all? A ring isn't a difficult thing to show in a dream; people are dreaming about rings all the time. So why not dream about a ring made of molecules, especially since the dream presented the molecules themselves realistically enough? I talked earlier about Level One non-symbolic dreams, and Level Two and Three symbolic ones (page 48). Symbolism is primarily the stuff of divergent, open-ended creative activity, so why doesn't the dream operate only at Level One when convergent, intelligent solutions are needed?

Dreams as a Way of Awakening the Mind

My answer is that for many dreams the unconscious *deliberately chooses to use symbols*. I mentioned earlier (pages 37 and 39) that psychodynamic psychologists see the symbol as a protective mechanism, designed either to defend the conscious mind from the unconscious (as emphasised by Freud), or to avoid exposing it too abruptly to deep truths about ourselves (as emphasised by Jung). But there is a further explanation. Freud and Jung tell us only part of the story. It seems overwhelmingly that the unconscious uses symbolism in dreams because it actively wants to set us puzzles in order to stimulate us into inquiry. To prompt our conscious minds to start working creatively. To goad consciousness into keeping pace with unconsciousness.

In the great spiritual traditions of the East, the theme of man being half asleep, unaware of who he is and of his destiny, is a constantly recurring one. The Rubaiyat of Omar Khayyam starts with the clarion call to 'Awake'!

> Awake! for Morning in the Bowl of Night
> Has flung the Stone that puts the Stars to Flight:
> And Lo! the Hunter of the East has caught
> The Sultan's Turret in a Noose of Light.

> Dreaming when Dawn's Left Hand was in the Sky
> I heard a Voice within the Tavern cry,
> 'Awake, my Little ones, and fill the Cup
> Before Life's Liquor in its Cup be dry.'

In the West we see the same theme in Jung's metaphor of the occupant of a splendid house never moving outside the basement, and of course it lay at the heart of Gurdjieff's system for spiritual development. For Gurdjieff, man had to be stung, provoked, shocked into awaking. Mere words wouldn't do it. Hence the bizarre, often apparently self-defeating tasks he set his pupils, reminiscent at times of the koan system in Zen Buddhism, another powerful system for waking the student from his or her dull, blinkered way of looking at the world.

It may seem strange that dreams could be there to help us wake up, when in ordinary thinking we use the term 'dreamer' precisely for the purpose of describing someone who is half asleep. But judging by the creative and intelligent 'leaps' that Kekulé and others are able to make in dreams this seems indeed to be the case; with symbolism, by its very other-worldly and intriguing nature, helping to make the dream memorable and to tease the receptive mind into effort and inquiry.

Other Examples of Problem Solving in Dreams

I return to the question of dream symbolism later in the chapter, but first some more examples of how dreams can help in problem solving. In 1619 when he was 23, Descartes, one of the prime founders of modern scientific thinking (and also, unwittingly, of much of the over-emphasis upon rationalism and positiveness which still bedevils it), had three particularly vivid dreams in quick succession one night which changed the whole course of his thinking. Already a gifted mathematician, Descartes was at the time turning to philosophy, and the three dreams involved a whirlwind, claps of thunder, and two books, one a dictionary and the other a book of poems. Descartes, a devout Christian, believed that in the dreams God showed him the whirlwind to drive him forward, the thunderclaps as a sign the spirit of truth had descended upon him, and the books to reveal that poetry as well as philosophy had a part to play in this truth.

From these dreams came the illumination for what Descartes believed to be his greatest discovery, namely the unity of all the human sciences. Notice again the symbolism, in this case biblical in content – the whirlwind, the thunder and the books. Less obviously biblical in character is a dream that Neils Bohr, the key figure in the genesis of modern atomic physics, is said to have had as a student. Bohr apparently dreamt he was standing on the surface of a sun, with planets whistling past, each of them attached to the sun by a thin filament. On awaking, he felt convinced that this was the long-sought model of the atom.

Accounts of Bohr's dream vary, and it is possible that he had more than one such dream around this time. But the interesting thing is that three of the founders of modern science, Kekulé in chemistry, Descartes in the philosophy of science, and Bohr in physics all apparently made their major breakthrough as the result of dreams.

Yet another example of a discovery that helped establish modern science was that of the nineteenth century Russian chemist Mendeleev, who after many fruitless attempts to tabulate the elements according to their atomic weights actually saw the required periodic table in a dream. Unlike the musicians and poets who struggle fruitlessly to recall dream inspiration he remembered every detail of the table on waking, and wrote it down just as he saw it. Only one of the values later proved to need correction.

Notice that Mendeleev's dream provides an instance of Level One, non-symbolic dreaming. This is consistent with the point I made a moment ago that the symbolism in dreams is a matter of choice. In Mendeleev's case it isn't easy to see how such an intricate table could be presented symbolically, so the unconscious apparently decided to give the information in undisguised form. On a personal (though I have to admit rather less spectacular) level than that of Mendeleev, in one of my own dreams I was presented quite out of the blue with the equation $3 \times 19 = 57$. Having no experience of the 19 times table I was intrigued on waking to know whether this was correct or not, and found on checking that it was. A small incident, but highly significant for me because it was clear evidence of the dream's ability to operate intelligently.

Turning away from the natural sciences, another good example of problem solving in dreams is that of Hilprecht, the renowned nineteenth century expert on early Middle-Eastern civilizations. Hilprecht had struggled all evening to decipher the inscriptions on two small fragments of agate which were supposedly parts of Babylonian finger-rings, and of which he only had a rough sketch. Giving up the fruitless task, he went to bed and dreamt in remarkable detail that a priest of the appropriate Babylonian period (circa 1300 BC) appeared to him and explained that the fragments of agate came not from rings but from a votive cylinder (presented by King Kurigalzu to the temple) which he and his fellow-priests had cut into three parts in order to furnish adornments for a statue of the god Ninib. The priest informed Hilprecht that the two fragments in the sketch were the two parts that had gone to provide the god's earrings, but that no fragment of the third part would ever be found.

Hilprecht was further instructed to put the two fragments together, and when on awaking he did so he was able to read from the rough sketch that, allowing for certain missing letters, they read in translation 'To the god Ninib, son of Bel, his Lord, has Kurigalzu, pontifex of Bel presented this.' Further confirmation came a few weeks later when Hilprecht was able to examine the actual agate fragments themselves (which had been catalogued separately by the museum holding them, as no-one had realised they belonged with each other) and discover that they fitted exactly together.

Another striking example comes from the German scientist Otto Loewi, who reported that the inspiration which led him to prove his theory of the chemical (as opposed solely to the electrical) transmission of nerve impulses came to him in a dream. In the dream he received the design of the necessary experiment, got up at once and performed it to his satisfaction on a frog's heart. He doesn't tell us whether the dream came to him in symbolic form or not, but we do know that as a result of the work inspired by it he received the 1936 Nobel Prize for Physiology and Medicine.

Other examples worthy of a mention (all Level One non-symbolic dreams) are Agassiz, the leading Swiss naturalist who in 1848 reconstructed the zoological characteristics of a fossil fish which had long puzzled him, after having twice previously had the same dream but found the details escaped him on waking; Fabré, an even more noted nineteenth century naturalist, who confessed to sleeping upon problems until 'a brilliant beacon flares up in my brain, and then I jump from my bed, light my lamp and write down the solution the memory of which would otherwise be lost'; and the German eighteenth century acoustics expert Chladni, who claimed that his invention of the tuba was due to a dream in which the instrument appeared to him and caused him such excitement that he awoke as if from an electric shock.

The Case Against Dreams as Forgetting

It is interesting to see from the dates for many of these dreams that at one time scientists appeared much less reluctant to discuss their dreams than they are now. It is even more interesting to look at these accounts and see how comprehensively they discount the *forgetting* explanation for dreaming (page 18). The dreams concerned may all have arisen out of intense intellectual struggles carried out during waking hours, but the point about them is that they went *beyond* these struggles, actually producing solutions which previously had proved unobtainable.

The extent to which Hilprecht's dream went beyond the limits of waking information is particularly impressive. To deny that it did so we would have to suppose that at some point in his waking life he had examined the two fragments of agate in their home in the museum, had realised that they had been wrongly catalogued as separate items, had put the two pieces together mentally or physically and decoded their inscriptions, and then not bothered to make this important discovery public. Not only that, we would also have to suppose that it had slipped completely from his conscious mind, and refused to resurface not only when faced with the rough sketch of the two pieces of agate but also, later, when faced with the two miscatalogued items themselves. Hilprecht's standing as a scholar makes this explanation unlikely, to say the very least.

But Hilprecht's case is important for yet another reason. *How* did his unconscious manage to make this giant leap beyond the information held in his conscious mind? Does this leap suggest to us that the dream can provide us with information which by no reasonable stretch of the imagination could be come by through normal means? An intriguing possibility, and one to which I return in Chapter 6 where the presence of ESP in dreams is discussed. For the moment, let's stay with problem solving, and then go on from there to see if there are ways we can actively encourage this kind of activity in our own dream life.

Here's another example of problem-solving in dreams, this time by a very remarkable woman, Pat Hunt, who has an outstanding gift in this direction and with whom I was privileged to work experimentally over many months. In one of our experiments Pat was presented with a series of very advanced intelligence test items such as complex anagrams and word and mathematical problems. In spite of a lively waking intelligence these were all problems to which she could find no conscious solution. She then held each problem in her mind as she drifted off to sleep, and (often at her first attempt but sometimes a night or two later) would have dreams which presented her with particularly vivid images. Free association to these images during waking hours over the following days led her to solutions which she could then check consciously against the original problems.

For example, when given the anagram SCNACEDELIHSKR she dreamt on the first night of one of the actresses who played in a TV series popular at the time called *Dempsey and Makepeace*. On waking, the dream meant nothing to her except that the actress had a distinctive hairstyle reminiscent of one of her friends called Carol. She also rembered that Carol had once said that she wished she looked like the actress playing Makepeace.

The following night the dream featured a Cairn terrier, which wanted to be carried. On waking, Pat was struck by the fact that both 'Cairn' and 'carried' start with the letters 'ca'. This suggested that the word 'Carol', which arose in association to the first dream and which starts with the same two letters, may have had particular significance...Carol wanted to be like Makepeace...Makepeace led to thoughts of 'peace on earth, goodwill towards men'...which suggested the idea of Christmas. Put *Christmas* and *Carol* together and the result is *Christmas Carol*. Charles Dickens wrote *A Christmas Carol*. Charles Dickens is the solution to the anagram.

This example is by no means the most outstanding, but it's short and easily described. It also gives the flavour of the whole series of experiments. Throughout these experiments the dream appeared to know the answer, but to prefer each time to present it in an enigmatic rather than a straightforward form. It left the waking mind to do some of the puzzling in a playful, almost provocative way. It also showed considerable ingenuity. Notice how in the example it chose a symbol – the actress in *Dempsey and Makepeace* – who carried a dual significance, both because she reminded the dreamer of the friend called 'Carol', and because she played the part of the person called 'Makepeace'. This suggests a high level of complexity in whatever thought processes are involved.

Among the many interesting features of this series of experiments was that, since the problems given to Pat demanded high-level intelligence for their solution, the dreaming mind was clearly able to operate at this level, thus providing us with further confirmation that dreams can be intelligent as well as creative. Another interesting feature is that the dream (or rather the unconscious as author of the dream) nevertheless 'chose' to present the solutions in a creative, symbolic form rather than in a straightforward intelligent one. This is further support for the idea that the dream characteristically wants to prompt the conscious mind into doing some of its own thinking – using a more convergent, analytical approach – rather than simply spoonfeed it with answers.

It could be objected, of course, that during these experiments the dreaming mind didn't do any of the problem solving, but that the unconscious recognised the answers to the problems *before* the dreamer actually went to sleep, and that the dreaming mind then had only to dramatise them. If this is indeed the case, it tells us something as exciting about the abilities of the unconscious mind during waking hours as does the dream about its abilities during sleep. But in my view we don't have to make a decision as to when the unconscious actually solved the problems. Rather, we should see the unconscious as a continuous process, operating without a break throughout the hours of waking and sleeping. The only difference is that during sleep, when the conscious mind ceases its chatter, we can pay more attention to it and to its workings. (Though what this 'attention' is, if it is neither the conscious mind itself nor the unconscious but something which can attend to either or both of them remains a mystery to psychology.)

Another possible objection to the idea that Pat's dreaming mind solved the problems during these experiments is that she *consciously* solved the problems while awake, but chose to keep the solutions to herself and then to invent the dream accounts with the deliberate intention of deceiving. In any work on dreaming, from the recording of simple accounts of dreams after REM sleep to work of the kind detailed here, it is impossible fully to rule out fraud on the part of the dreamer – or for that matter on the part of the experimenter. Dreams are private, personal knowledge, and we have to rely upon the dreamer's own accounts of them. In the present case I have complete faith in the integrity of the dreamer, and an equal faith in my own determination not to mislead my readers.

Problem Solving in Your Dreams

The dreamer I worked with in the above experiments is blessed with great natural ability in the use of her dreams, and the procedure she uses she developed for herself and without any assistance from previous reading or research. But the main technique for opening oneself to the problem-solving abilities of the dreaming mind have long been recognised (though not, regrettably, by orthodox Western psychology). Let's run through it. It's intended specifically for clear-cut problems which have a convergent, intelligent, single right answer. I deal with techniques for more general problems of relationship and personal growth in Chapter 5.

1. Allow the waking mind to study the problem as much as it likes in its attempt to find a solution. Don't be too intense about it. As with most instances when we try to engage deeper levels of our mind, a curiosity-based, almost playful approach is better than a fierce, do-or-die one.

2. When it's finally clear that the solution is not coming, put the problem out of your conscious mind if you can, but in an

optimistic, 'I know the solution is bound to come' frame of mind rather than a defeated one.

3. Each time the problem re-enters your mind, tell yourself confidently that you needn't bother with it now because you know you'll solve it later, during your dreams.

4. When you go to bed, hold the problem lightly in your mind, *but making no attempt to solve it.* Try to keep it there as you drift off to sleep.

5. On waking, write down at once any dream you can recall. Don't study it first to see if it has relevance to your problem, simply write it down, in as much detail as you can.

6. Once you've recorded everything you can from the night's adventures, identify all the major images that cropped up. Free associate to them by asking yourself what they suggest to you.

7. Return to this exercise whenever you can during the day. Keep your mind open and free of anxiety. If the solution doesn't come easily, tell yourself it doesn't matter because you'll have a clearer dream that night.

8. Be patient. Don't dismiss the exercise because the answer doesn't come the first night. And don't tell yourself that your message to your dreaming mind wasn't strong enough to get through. You may have dreamt the solution early in the night and forgotten the dream by morning. Or the solution may be there in your remembered dream, and so far you haven't teased it out. Tell yourself that it will be given to you more plainly tonight.

If you don't have specific problems to work on, ask someone to give you a difficult anagram on which to work. Or a mathematical puzzle. Problems of this kind, where the right answer already exists and where you can keep checking your own solution against the original problem provide excellent practice. Once the technique starts to work for you, your dreaming mind should become more sensitive to real-life problems as well.

BOX 6
MORE ON PROBLEM-SOLVING IN DREAMS

If you find that, in spite of using the technique I've described, you still can't problem-solve in dreams, start inventing 'problem-solving' dreams for yourself.

Do this by following steps 1 to 3 of the technique as shown, but when you get to bed, not only hold the problem in your mind (step 4) but also think up the scenario for a dream in which the solution to the problem could be given.

Make the scenario as strange and unusual as you like. Remember that dreams like to operate in this way. In your scenario, you don't have to try and approach the solution. Simply set the scene, and let your dreaming mind do the rest.

For example, if you are working on a mathematical problem, imagine yourself in a shop, with the shop assistant counting out some change into your hand. Or playing snooker and making a long break, with the referee calling out your score as you go along. Or looking at a time-chart and flicking back through the years. Use whatever scenario fits best with your interests. Don't concentrate on any particular numbers, just on the idea of numbers themselves.

If you are using an anagram, imagine a crossword puzzle. See the blank spaces and imagine yourself filling them in. If you prefer, imagine the letters of the alphabet coming to life and running around a room until suddenly they start to organise themselves into words. Or imagine yourself playing a word game such as scrabble. Once again, don't concentrate in any of these scenarios on actual letters or words, just on the idea of them.

Your imaginary dream may not produce an actual dream which uses the same scenario or even the same images (although it may), but the concentration upon numbers or letters – or upon whatever is the dominant feature of the problem you're trying to solve – will help stimulate a dream focused in the right direction. After your night's sleep, proceed with steps 5 to 8 of the techniques as given.

Another approach to problem-solving is to look at one of your incorrect solutions and ask the dream to tell you why it's wrong. Keep in mind before you go off to sleep the idea of a *misfit* between this solution and the correct one. Imagine the incorrect solution standing in one place (visualise it as a person if you like, or as printed upon a card, or whichever way seems most helpful) and the correct solution in another. You can't see the details of the correct solution, but you watch it move over and take the place of the incorrect one.

Remember in all this work the golden rules of *confidence* and *patience*.

4

BETWEEN WAKING
AND SLEEPING

At this point we need to look at a phenomenon closely related to dreams, and one which we must understand if we're fully to explore our potential for making use of our dream lives. In order to take this look, we have to return to the actual business of falling asleep.

Although we're not certain as to the precise function of sleep, at an informal level most people feel that during sleep their minds take a rest from the stress of waking life. This rest begins even before we actually sink into the first phase of our sleep cycle. In the moments between waking and sleeping, as we begin to lose touch with the world around us without yet showing the physiological changes of sleep itself, we go through a strange half-way house known as the *hypnogogic* state in which the mind presents us with a series of brief, hallucinatory images. In its elusive, enchanted quality this state rivals dreaming itself, and for many practical purposes we can indeed treat it as a form of dreaming. Over the last two decades it has attracted increasing research attention in sleep laboratories, and we now have considerable evidence as to its nature.

In the hypnogogic state, we experience not so much the story-making experience of the dream proper (though this can happen) as a succession of disconnected fleeting pictures, some of them possessing a curious vivid beauty. If you feel you have never experienced this state, recall a time when you were suddenly aroused just as you were dropping off to sleep. You will most probably remember you were in the middle of some particularly delightful thoughts, yet frustratingly were unable to recall exactly what they were. You maybe struggled to hold on to the last fragments of their memory, yet in the moment of grasping them they finally and irrevocably eluded you. This was an experience of being aroused from the hypnogogic state.

There is a similar half-way house as we climb up each morning from sleeping to waking. Known this time as the *hypnopompic* state, it's characterised by the same vivid, disconnected images (though I for one am not alert enough in the mornings to be properly aware of them, and have to take their existence rather on trust). Research shows that the hypnogogic and the hypnopompic states are so much alike that there is probably no need to have two separate names for them. So from now on I shall refer only to the hypnogogic, and everything I say will apply equally to both of them.

Hypnogogic Imagery

The intriguing thing about much hypnogogic imagery is its involuntary nature. One bright image follows another, without any apparent association between them, and without any obvious links to one's waking experiences. In my own case, for example, I may see a river flowing through a beautiful green landscape of hills and distant mountains, followed by a solitary man seen in profile sitting under a tree, followed by the rooftops of houses in a strange town, followed by boats on a canal and so on. None of these images relate to any place I've been or any picture I can remember seeing. My mind creates them in all their richness, without any apparent contribution from my conscious thought processes. One moment there is nothing there behind my closed eyelids, and the next an image leaps up, ready made, as if setting the stage in a magic picture show.

I seem to 'see' the images with my left eye rather than with my right, which suggests a connection with the right hemisphere of the brain (see page 22). Sometimes the images are preceded by, though usually unconnected with, similar phenomena at the auditory level. That is, by verbalisations, which like snatches of overheard conversation leap from nowhere into my mind. Mostly they deal with trivial matters which have nothing directly to do with me. A comment about the weather. An observation about a book. A description of a place. But they come with a clarity comparable to that of the visual experiences, and seem to arise from the same source. For some people there can also be bodily sensations at this time, such as a feeling of floating or flying, and sometimes the body gives a sudden jerk, as if falling, which often seems to be in direct response to one or other of the visual or auditory experiences.

The visual and auditory hypnogogic experiences are similar to those that sometimes arise in meditation, suggesting that in both conditions the mind briefly touches similar levels. So meditators as well as those interested in dreams sometimes ask whether there are techniques which can make us more aware of such experiences and help us further develop their richness (and possible usefulness). The answer is that yes there are, and that such techniques are a valuable lead-in to the use and control of dreams themselves.

Becoming Aware of Hypnogogic Images

These techniques all depend upon something that sounds deceptively simple but can prove remarkably difficult, namely maintaining awareness into the hypnogogic state and watching what happens during it. More research is needed on how people settle down to sleep at night, but a common pattern for most of us is to think for a few minutes about the events of the day until, lulled by the comfort of the bed and the relaxed state of the body, we allow sleep to take over. After the first few minutes, the process becomes an involuntary one. We don't have to *do* anything to fall asleep; sleep comes of its own accord.

There is nothing wrong with any of this, and we shouldn't try every night to change these pleasant habits. Some people find they can consciously will themselves to sleep, but for most of us the conscious mind is an intruder at this time. Nevertheless, if we want to use our dreams, we need gradually to introduce some elements of control into the process of falling asleep. As we shall see in Chapter 8, the more mystical schools of Tibetan Buddhism place particular emphasis upon this as a necessary step in our psycho-spiritual development, and even teach, as I said earlier, that falling asleep constitutes a dress rehearsal for death. By gaining conscious control over the process, we are told, it is possible to learn how to control our dying and thus how to control what happens to us in the after-life.

The essential element in gaining this control is to watch more closely the process as it unfolds. As this often leads to a prolonged period of wakefulness in the beginner, let me stress again that you shouldn't try to do it every night. You don't want to turn yourself into an insomniac. Two or three times a week is enough. And when you attempt it, for goodness sake don't lie there in gritted determination, forcing yourself come what may to be attentive. This destroys the whole object of the exercise. In this wakeful, ego-dominated state, hypnogogic images will never arise. What you're aiming to do is to drift off to sleep as usual, yet to allow part of your mind to watch the process unfold. This part of the mind is going to be overtaken by sleep just like all the rest, but not until the last moment.

So settle yourself for sleep, stop thinking about anything special, and allow a kind of relaxed alertness to remain. I find it particularly helpful to place my awareness behind my closed eyelids, as if I'm patiently watching for something to happen, but not minding too much if it doesn't. Other people like to place their awareness between and above the eyes, in the place of the 'third eye' of yoga. The heart region is another possibility, so is the crown of the head.

These last three positions are of course three of the chakra regions, the non-physical energy centres taught in yoga philosophy, and you can use any of the other such centres if you prefer. It is sometimes said that the kind of visions you have will depend upon which of them you choose. If you choose the lower chakras in the perineum and the abdomen you will have sensual visions, and if you choose the crown of the head you will have exalted ones. These are very much matters for personal exploration, but to begin with the eyes themselves, or the 'third eye', are good places. The most important thing, as in meditation, is simply to have a place upon which to focus the mind.

Let's assume you choose the eyes. Make sure that the eye muscles are perfectly relaxed (most of us put far more energy into keeping our eyes closed than we need), and just look into the darkness. The first few nights you try this, you'll probably drift off to sleep before anything happens. Don't be discouraged. As is said of meditation, time means nothing in work of this kind. Results may take a while to come, but this doesn't mean you're not going to get them. Persevere. Success in this sort of endeavour is often directly proportional to the strength of your motivation. Be patient.

Maybe the first time you try, maybe the second or the third, maybe the ninth or tenth, maybe the hundredth, you will suddenly become conscious of an image appearing. Never try to force it to do so. You can easily *make* yourself imagine something, but this is a conscious effort, just like our attempt to imagine something when fully awake. The point about a hypnogogic image is that it suddenly appears, ready made, like a fish leaping out of water. There is no mistaking the difference between it and something you put there consciously.

At first the image may be very faint, so fleeting you might easily miss it. Don't expect something vivid and brightly-coloured right from the word go. (You *may* be lucky, but more likely you may not.) Or your first experience may be of words, like the overheard snatches of conversation I mentioned earlier. Whichever it is, don't try to hang on to it or prolong it. Don't think about it and start speculating as to what it might or might not mean. Don't scrutinise it too closely or try and examine it for minute detail. If you do you'll lose it at once. Simply observe it. Don't get excited about it. Don't judge it. See it and let it go, which it will do all too soon.

After a few of these images, you will probably drift off to sleep. Fine. There's nothing to be gained by deliberately trying to prolong the hypnogogic state. As like as not, all that will happen is that in your efforts to do so you will bring yourself fully awake, and once you wake from this state it is often very hard indeed to re-enter it and to go beyond it into sleep.

With practice, it becomes possible not only to observe the hynogogic state but to remember some of the images contained in it even when you wake the following morning. You may not necessarily remember all the details, but you will at least remember the settings. Don't, by the way, think that by observing the images you are somehow 'creating' this state. It happens anyway, every night. The only difference now is that instead of being too close to sleep to notice it, part of your mind is still aware.

If you have trouble in establishing an awareness of the hypnogogic state, put more emphasis upon the point at which you're directing your awareness. In one of the Tibetan traditions, the teaching is to imagine a spinning disc of light at this awareness point. (The heart chakra is the point particularly recommended for this purpose.) After visualising this disc, images will start to flash through it. Just observe them, and in the intervals between them return to your contemplation of the spinning disc. Hypnogogic images can sometimes be induced in the waking state by the technique of scrying, that is by staring at a polished surface or into a bowl of water stained with black ink or into a crystal ball, and the spinning disc of light is an imaginary and very potent substitute for aids of this kind.

Another technique is to keep at the centre of your awareness, gently and without effort, the name of an object you would like to see. A red rose perhaps, or a broad river, or a snow-capped mountain. Don't try and 'create' the image for yourself. Simply think of it in an abstract way. When the image appears, it will often be different in detail from the one in your mind. The red rose might turn out to be a pink or yellow one, the broad river a rushing stream or a waterfall, the snow-capped mountain a green hill topped by a pine forest. Or a different image altogether might appear. Don't experience surprise. Simply observe what happens.

A further suggestion is to practise observing numbers or the letters of the alphabet in sequence, in the colour of your choice and on a contrasting background (blue on white perhaps, gold on black, yellow on blue – don't choose something too arousing like red on green or something that clashes like green on blue). This may prompt images which have to do with letters or numbers, but it can be a useful way of getting the practice established.

But whatever the technique employed, it is important to feel in a detached way that although we know the images are simply a product of our own minds, they are nevertheless 'real' in the sense that they deserve our attention. To begin with you may see abstract geometric shapes rather than anything concrete, but give them this same sense of worth. As with all dream work, the more *relaxed* importance we attach to what takes place, the more available it becomes to us.

Dealing With Unpleasant Images

Of course, like dreams themselves, not all hypnogogic images are pleasant ones. Sometimes you may see threatening faces or dark gloomy scenes. View them with the same sense of detached interest. Life itself presents us with unpleasant as well as pleasant scenes, and we cannot expect either in hypnogogy or in dreams always to escape the former. To be able to see the unpleasant images without fear or alarm is good practice. The Tibetans teach that they are similar to the wrathful deities that we see in the bardo state after death, and that by confronting them instead of fleeing from them we enhance the control that we have over this state.

Should the unpleasant images prove particularly persistent however, don't make the mistake of trying too hard to push them away. This only communicates to the unconscious the fact that they have strong negative significance for you and, in the perverse way with which the unconscious deals with such matters, succeeds in strengthening them (see Box 7). The technique for banishing them is to focus upon something which is abstract and as unlike them as possible. A geometric shape for example, preferably in the form of a mandala which has positive associations for you. Don't consciously try and construct the shape for yourself. Keep the mind in its detached state, and simply suggest to it what you want to see, and then wait for it to emerge.

But, helpful as working upon the hypnogogic state undoubtedly is as a preliminary to understanding and using your dreams, it isn't essential. If the negative hypnogogic images persist and become frightening, it's better therefore to give this state a miss for the time being. You can return to it later, when you have gained more understanding of your dream life, and found you have the power to banish even the much more frightening images that arise from time to time in dreaming itself. Once you have made this discovery, it isn't difficult to come back to hypnogogy and continue the banishing exercise.

We don't have direct evidence on what effect banishing frightening images from hypnogogy has upon our psychological development. But as working on our dreams is such a valuable psychological practice it's right to suppose that working on hypnogogic states is also helpful (and see Box 7 again). As I've already said, by becoming aware of these states we are not actually creating them. They are there anyway. All we're doing is bringing them into conscious awareness. Consistently seeing frightening images in this state may, like consistently seeing frightening images in dreams, show that we have some unconscious fears which need to be dealt with at one level or another.

But the main value of working with the hypnogogic state is that it puts us progressively into closer touch with our unconscious. It's a way of beginning to explore some of those other rooms in our splendid mansion. Our unconscious throws up these images. Why? What do they mean to us? And why these particular images and not others? One view advanced by the orthodox theories on dreaming discussed in Chapter 2 is that, as the onset of sleep makes us increasingly oblivious to the signals received from our senses, so the brain tries desperately to keep in touch with the outside world by inventing its own sights and sounds. Another is that the images are simply the result of our brain cells continuing to fire off their signals, in a random and disjointed way as we drop off to sleep. Rather like the way in which sometimes a car engine goes on firing for a moment or two after we switch off the ignition.

However, as with dreaming, anyone who takes the trouble to study this state for themselves quickly becomes aware of the poverty of this kind of explanation. Like dreams, the hypnogogic images are creative. They go beyond the information given. Rather than consisting merely of odd bits of form or colour put together haphazardly from the day's experiences, they present us with something new and coherent. We see breathtaking scenery we've never seen before, we see people and images, we see events taking place. The master artist in each one of us puts together a visual spectacular, a spectacular which, if we attend to it, takes us into deeper and deeper (or higher and higher) reaches of our own being.

BOX 7
**MORE ABOUT THE FUNCTION OF THE
HYPNOGOGIC STATE**

Research into the hypnogogic state shows that for many
people even the most frightening images fail to produce an
unpleasant reaction. Such people report they feel a surprising
lack of emotional response to these images, either at the time
or afterwards. They speak of a 'detached involvement'. They
are drawn to the images, yet view them as if from a position
beyond the normal world of petty anxieties and tensions. This
leads some authorities on the hypnogogic state to argue that
part of its purpose is to act as an anxiety-reducer. It's there to
show us that we don't really have to be terrified by the
pictures with which life presents us. We can look upon the
most disturbing scenes with equanimity and without the
feeling that we must escape from them. And we can survey
the most beautiful ones with serenity and without the feeling
that we must grasp and hold onto them.

   Allied to this is the fact that, in the hypnogogic state, both
body and brain often achieve high degrees of relaxation.
Skeletal muscles lose their tension, and the blood lactate
produced by this tension (and which when present can send
anxiety-promoting signals to the brain) falls markedly. What
psychologists call our 'threshold of excitability' (the level at
which we begin to feel nervously aroused and tense) is also
raised significantly, so that feelings of unease in response to
usually unpleasant stimuli from the body or from the mind
become less likely to arise. Thus at both physical and mental
levels the hypnogogic state helps renew our energies, and
restore and regenerate us for what tomorrow is going to bring.

*...And About Strengthening Negative Images By Pushing
Them Away*
It's a strange fact – but one of which most of us are well
aware – that the more you try to push away unpleasant
thoughts and feelings the harder they cling to you. Why is
this? A clue lies in the way in which, when we've had one or
two more drinks than we can handle, we're apt to say things
to our friends (or even complete strangers) that shock and hurt
them. In the cold light of dawn we're aghast about it and
wonder what came over us. Do these remarks reflect the
things we *really* feel about our friends? Does losing our
inhibitions under the influence of alcohol mean that we show
our true nature, in all its unpleasantness? By no means. What
happens is that the very few negative things we may feel
about our friends, but which out of sensitivity or politeness we

BOX 7
MORE ABOUT THE FUNCTION OF THE
HYPNOGOGIC STATE

refrain from saying, gain a kind of frustrated energy by being
constantly repressed. When we're somewhat in our cups, they
then burst out with all the force of this frustration, rather as a
river which has been dammed surges through a sudden
breach in the dam wall. If we had been able to say these
things when we first felt them, they would have emerged like
innocent chance remarks, with no more energy than remarks
about the weather.

   Pushing away unpleasant thoughts or unpleasant
hypnogogic images has the same effect as damming a river.
We build up their energy by showing that we can't face them,
just as we build up the energy behind the things we feel we
must refrain from saying to our friends. The answer is to just
let them be. If they want to be there, okay. But they don't
really merit our attention. Like the weather, just observe them,
then leave them to their own devices.

   In the hypnogogic state what we might call the 'filters' that
operate when we are fully awake, and which prevent much of
the material not directly relevant to our waking concerns from
getting through into consciousness, are removed. If we doubt
the creative power of these images, and their capacity for
disturbing and engaging us, for filling us with a strange feeling
that somehow we have visited all these places before, that we
know what they mean, although we can't quite remember what
this meaning is, look at surrealistic art. The surrealists were
very influenced by their dreams, but perhaps even more by the
hypnogogic visions. In their paintings we see echoes of these
visions, strange enigmatic landscapes, the imposition of fantasy
upon reality or of reality upon fantasy, an entry into another
world that is frightening, hauntingly beautiful, enigmatic, and
yet somehow familiar. Our own inner world, closer than the
view from the bedroom window or than the four walls within
which we sleep.

5

YOUR DREAMS
AND THEIR MEANING

We're now at the point where we can start interpreting our own dreams. If you've been working on remembering your dreams and have started keeping a dream diary, you should also have some useful material with which to start. It's perfectly possible – and often desirable – to interpret individual dreams, but if you have several to look at this is even better. Often you can identify patterns and recurring themes across them, and these indicate your unconscious has particular preoccupations which need investigating.

In Chapter 2, I looked at the ways in which dreams have been interpreted across the centuries, and paid particular attention to four modern Western psychological approaches, those of Freud, Jung, Perls and Boss. Between them, these four approaches give a comprehensive picture of the way in which dreams can be encouraged to yield up their meaning, and we can use a combination of them in our own work. Remember that in Chapter 2, I said that dreams operate on a number of different levels. This means that any approach to dreaming which sticks rigidly to just one level cannot give us a full picture, and if applied too dogmatically can even mislead us altogether.

BOX 8
DREAM SYMBOLISM

The world is full of symbols. A symbol is simply something that stands for something else. Words themselves are symbols, and so are numbers. Most of the time we use symbols *denotively*. The word 'dog' stands for the animal dog, the number '100' stands for a specific quantity. But symbols can also be used *metaphorically*. The word 'dog' can stand for a person of bad behaviour, the number '100' can stand for a landmark in a batsman's innings or a snooker player's visit to the table. Unlike denotive symbols which convey something definite, metaphorical symbols carry a complex of meanings and attitudes usually at a subjective mental level, and it is metaphorical symbols that interest us in dreams.

The reason for this interest is precisely because they represent such a complex of meanings and attitudes, some of which we are well aware of at the conscious waking level, but others of which lie unacknowledged in the unconscious. Unlocking the hidden meaning behind these symbols therefore gives us an insight into the unconscious.

Metaphorical symbols may be personal to ourselves (a particular design of armchair may symbolise old age for you because your grandmother always used one), or we may share them with most of our fellows ('high' is a universal symbol for success, 'low' for failure). It is these shared symbols that are of particular interest. Jung, as we saw in Chapter 2, sees them as giving access to the collective unconscious, and in Tantric and alchemical practice they are seen as the keys to higher levels of consciousness.

Working With Dream Symbols
There are two major ways of working with dream symbols. The first is to study your dream diary for their appearance. Take for example the symbols known as archtypes. We first met these archetypes on page 40. Jung tells us that among the most important in dreams are the *shadow* (our own dark side, represented by an enigmatic or hostile person), the *child* (primordial innocence and wisdom), the *hero* (our ideal self), the *wise old man* (acquired wisdom) the *mother* (creativity, the unconscious), and the *maiden* (beauty, truth). But archetypes can also be in the form of things not experienced in waking life such as dragons, helpful animals, gods, hidden treasure, strange masks and alchemical processes. Archetypal *situations* also exist, such as flying through space, becoming the sun, moon or earth, dying, or becoming a stranger to oneself. Archetypal dreams are Level Three dreams, and Jung claims they can always be recognised by their cosmic, deeply significant feeling.

BOX 8
DREAM SYMBOLISM

The second way is to choose a particular symbol as a focus for meditation then watch for it's appearance in your dreams. Look at a picture of it or visualise it. The mandalas used in Eastern religions are ideal, as are alchemical symbols. So is the Celtic cross, or the geometrical shapes I suggested you use in the hypnogogic state (page 70). Stick to the same symbol. Frequent change hinders progress. This way of working with symbols is more relevant for the techniques discussed in Chapter 8.

The three levels I identified are:

Level One: The Non-Symbolic Level
Level Two: The Mundane Symbolic Level
Level Three: The Higher Symbolic Level.

Of these levels, Level Three dreams are the rarest, and can be recognised by the great impression they make upon us both at the time and after waking. Often these dreams stay undimmed in the mind for years, and may leave you with feelings of great peace and tranquillity (or with feelings that they represent some kind of unfinished business which you must at all costs come to understand and resolve). Jung called them 'great dreams', and identified them as invariably carrying archetypal images (see Box 8). Once you begin to work on your dreams (and generally on your psychological and spiritual growth) these dreams may become more frequent, though there is great individual variation in these matters.

In the same way there are marked individual variations between the relative frequency with which we each of us experience Level One and Level Two dreams. Some people have a preponderance of Level One dreams, others of Level Two. We mustn't enter into judgement about this, seeing for example anyone who has frequent Level Two dreams as being more psychologically or spiritually 'advanced' than the person whose dreaming takes place mainly at Level One. The variables involved are much too complex (and obscure) for us to make snap evaluations of this kind.

Single and Multi-Level Dreams

Some dreams work at only one of the levels, others may contain elements of all three. As I discussed in Chapter 3, dreams operate intelligently and creatively (and ingeniously, as we shall see in this chapter), and they can introduce a particular image and then proceed to use it at all three levels. In your dream work, don't necessarily stick at a single interpretation therefore. It may be perfectly correct, but go on working with the dream image to see if it carries further meaning.

On the other hand, don't feel that an image *must* carry more than one interpretation. If you have one interpretation that feels right, and nothing else comes up, then the chances are there is only one level of meaning with which to concern yourself.

In all work of this kind, the golden rule is that the interpretation must feel right to you. This doesn't mean you're free to manipulate it until it comes up smelling of roses. You have to be honest with yourself. Not all dreams tell us the kind of things we want to hear. But what it does mean is that if an interpretation, however obvious at face value, doesn't seem relevant to your life situation, then it probably isn't the right one.

Remember that dreams are a product of the unconscious, so they don't have to carry their meaning in the logical, rational way of the conscious mind. (Though as we saw in Chapter 3, they *can* give their information in this way if they choose.) So when interpreting them, put your mind into a free-wheeling playful mode, simply allowing whatever wants to emerge from the unconscious, however outlandish, to do so. It may be rubbish or it may not be. Take everything at its face value, until you've got a number of responses to the dream and can then begin to examine each one more closely.

Remember also that in work of this kind you must be patient. The dream may not reveal its meaning at first go. If it doesn't, keep it in your mind over the following days. Return to it in your thoughts whenever you can, not with a grim 'I *will* solve it' mentality, but in an open, intrigued, curious frame of mind – 'What *does* it mean, I wonder?'

Since dreams are a product of our creativity, enlist your other creative powers to help your interpretation. Draw or paint your dreams. If you enjoy music, make up a tune that seems to represent the dream. If you like words, write a line or two of poetry. Try modelling the significant dream images in clay. Speak to the dream. Ask it directly what it means. If the answer doesn't emerge, ask it to make its meaning clearer in the dreams you're going to have tonight. Although dreams seem to like to set us puzzles, there's no reason for thinking they want the answer to remain forever obscure. This would destroy the main purpose of dreaming. Dreams can hardly help us towards wholeness, to put our unconscious and our conscious minds in communication with each other, if all they want to do is baffle and confuse.

Steps in Dream Interpretation

With these important points in mind, you're ready to begin the process of interpretation. Let's assume for the moment that you're not trying to interpret any one particular dream, but are looking across a number of dreams to see if there are identifiable patterns. Study your dream diary and make notes of:

* Recurring dreams; some people dream largely the same dream either on several consecutive nights or regularly over a longer period.

* Recurring images and themes; look for the same people cropping up in dreams (are they strangers or people known to you? what role are they taking?), or the same kind of situations, or the same emotions.

* Dream events which make a particular impact (happy, frightening, puzzling) on you; also dream characters.

* The feelings and thoughts with which dreams leave you on waking, even if these have no obvious connection with the dreams themselves.

* The *quality* of your dreams; are they diverse and interesting? exciting? dull? menacing? long? short? coherent? disconnected? erotic?

* The dream scenery; is it of familiar or unfamiliar places? of town or country? are there dominant colours? are they bright or dark?

It's helpful to draw up a table, with dream images and events listed down the left, and the frequency with which each occurs entered in columns.

If you're interpreting a single dream, the procedure is the same except that now you're looking not for patterns across dreams but for things that strike you within just one. Identify each of the things that stand out in the dream – events, images, people, colours. Identify the thoughts and emotions experienced within the dream and immediately upon waking (this shows how important it is to record these things in your dream diary before they have a chance to fade). Identify the general *impression* conveyed by the dream – exciting, dull, coherent, incoherent and so on.

Write all these things down, preferably in your dream diary immediately underneath the account of the dream itself. Have them in front of you when you start your interpretation.

Level One Interpretation

Once you have gone through your dream diary or your individual dream in this way, pick out those themes and aspects which occur with particular frequency and/or which seem to you (for whatever reason) to be significant. Work on them first of all at Level One. Do they have meaning for you at face value? (Remember the example of Level One dream interpretation I gave from the work of Boss, page 45). Perhaps these significant dream happenings tell you something about the world and how you see it. Are they:

* optimistic or pessimistic?

* indicative of a broad or narrow life?

* confident or fearful, sure or unsure?

* evidence for individuality or conventionality?

* colourful or drab?

* orientated towards male or female images and events?

* peaceful or violent?

And so on. Work on the assumption your dreams are trying to tell you something. Even if your life is happy and successful, there will be things about it that could usefully be changed, aspects of your potential or the potential of others that you are neglecting, emotions you are repressing or denying, ambitions or goals from which you have perhaps wrongly turned away. Don't expect your dreams always to dwell on the light and positive side of life. Don't be afraid of what they have to tell you. For example, as I shall show in due course, even a pattern of violent dream images doesn't mean you're a violent person (nor does a pattern of erotic dreams mean you're over-sexed!).

Because we describe Level One dreaming as non-symbolic, this doesn't mean that everything at this level simply features things as they are in real life. Even at Level One, the dream is a dramatisation, not a representation. But at Level One the meaning is straightforward and clear, and doesn't require symbolic interpretation. So if, for example, the pattern that emerges at Level One is of a life lacking in certain of the things you feel it should contain, and if this pattern fits your own life when you come to reflect carefully upon it, then this pattern is the one the dream is trying to convey.

When you've looked at what the dreams may be telling you about the general pattern of your life, look more closely at some of the individual dream happenings. With each one, think of it as simply being what it seems to be. If you dream of losing a sum of money for example, this may show you have a specific anxiety about financial loss, or a more general fear (and insecurity) about losing the things you value. Try this interpretation and see if it fits. If you have a dream about success, this may show you prize success or are anxious to achieve success. Again try obvious non-symbolic interpretations like this and see if they fit.

Work on your dreams at Level One until you feel you have identified all they have to say to you at this non-symbolic level. Then go on to Level Two.

Level Two Interpretation

I've already said that some dreams may reveal all their meaning at Level One. So don't feel they have to carry a symbolic meaning as well. Just explore them to see. If after a while nothing of value emerges, leave it at that. Go back to Level One, and see if there are any further areas of non-symbolic meaning that remain to be explored.

In working at Level Two, the respective methods of Freud, Jung and Perls are all relevant. All three, in their rather different ways, produce legitimate results. So at first experiment with all three. If, as you develop your experience, you find that one of them produces better results for you than the other two, own it as your personal technique and use it in preference to the other two. Only revert to one or other of these if you reach a block when working on a particular dream. The change of technique usually gets you through the block.

Free association. The best method with which to start as a beginner is free association, since this is easy and (usually!) fun to use, and helps to open up the flow of creative, intuitive ideas so necessary in dreamwork. In order to free associate, take one of the significant aspects that emerges from your dream diary or from an individual dream – it may be a person, an event, a colour, a feeling, an object – and hold it in your mind. Play with it. Mentally turn it over and study it from every angle. Don't dissect it though. Keep it whole, just as it is.

Now – what comes into your mind as a result? a picture? an idea? a word? Don't judge it or examine it or wonder why. Just hold it in your mind. What comes next? Another picture, another idea, another word? Hold that in your mind and see what it suggests. Now see what *that* suggests and so on.

Each association suggests another association which suggests another and so on. Allow the mind to free-wheel, following this train of ideas. Don't interfere. Don't wonder why you should be getting so far away from the original dream image. Just follow the train until it arrives at something which seems significant to you or which carries a special emotional impact. It might be a sudden flash of awareness about yourself, a new insight into a problem, a memory from way back, a hidden emotion or attitude or prejudice about something, or a new kind of understanding about some aspect of life itself.

Sometimes, instead of reaching this point, the associations just peter out. You can't think of anything else, yet you don't feel you've reached anywhere that matters. If this is the case you can return to the dream image and start again, or you can take another of your dream images and start from there, or you can regard this as a block, a defence mechanism which is preventing you from going any deeper, and to which you should return again and again until suddenly you break through and pick up the train of associations again. Only you can decide which of these three courses of action is appropriate, and you must decide on the strength of the intuitive feeling you have about it rather than upon any attempt at rationalisation.

Let's take an example of free association in action. Starting with the image 'swing', one dreamworker came up with:

> circle, round, grace, beauty, harmony, eternal, everlasting, globe, earth, world, kingdom, cabbala, mysticism, secrets, hidden, wonders, meaning, answer, rightness, justice, mercy, the foundation and kether, the crown.

Readers familiar with mysticism will recognise the cabbalistic symbolism here – kingdom, cabbala, justice, mercy, the foundation and kether, the crown – but the important thing for the dreamer is the way the associations reveal a concern with the higher nature of things. This concern may already be recognised in waking life. Free association often leads us back to what we already know, and re-emphasises for us its vital importance. Or it may be something which the dreamer has been trying to hide from himself. Either way, the train of associations leads to a significant point.

In this example, the dreamer follows a train of nouns. But the train may instead take the form of memories and events. For example 'swing' could prompt the idea of the swinging sixties, which could lead to memories of the colourful clothes of the time, to the Beatles, to a pop festival, to flower power, to an experiment with LSD, to an affair with a girl that the dreamer left unconsummated, to sexual hang-ups and so on.

Free association works so well for most people, that you may wonder why we need to bother with the alternative approaches to dream interpretation of Jung and Perls. The answer is that although free association is a very powerful technique indeed for putting us in touch with ourselves, and for uncovering our concerns, our unconscious complexes, our psychological problems, our strengths and weaknesses, it may lead us away from the dream. In other words, it may tell us something very significant about ourselves, but this may not be the something very significant which the dream was trying to convey.

You can test this by taking any word at random from a dictionary and free associating to it. If you're able to put your mind into a sufficiently receptive state, the exercise may well lead you deep into your repressed self. As Jung puts it, 'from any point of the compass you can reach the centre directly'. But the word with which you started may have nothing to do with the particular place within the centre at which you end up. So entering this repressed self through free associations to a dream image may, for all its great value, fail to unlock the real meaning of the image itself. The image may provide you only with a starting point, of no greater significance in itself than the word taken at random from the dictionary. By using dream images in this way, you risk losing the messages which they really contain – though of course you may not always do so. You yourself are the best judge.

Amplification. The Jungian approach tries to avoid this risk of loss by using the powers of association in a rather different way. It gives more status to the dream by assuming that it is not really a disguise but means what it says – provided you can recognise what the symbols it uses are actually saying. Jung's method is a way of elaborating upon, or as he preferred to call it *amplifying* (or using *direct association* to) the dream image. Experiment with amplification once you have loosened up your responding with the necessary practice at free association. Let's see how amplification works.

Select your dream image as in free association, and once more hold it in your mind just as before. Look at it from every angle. Now what comes into your mind? Look at this new image in turn, but *don't allow it to spark off a train of associations that take you away from the dream*. Keep coming back to the dream. Keep the dream image in the centre of your awareness. Build up a constellation of associations around it, rather than a train of associations leading away from it.

For example, also starting from the dream image of a swing, but using amplification instead of free association, a dream-worker came up with the following:

child's plaything, garden, sunlight, swinging backwards and forwards in space, feelings of freedom and lightness, sounds of children's voices in the evening, my father pushing me on the swing, rising and falling, making progress then falling back, my father's safe hands always pushing me up again, enjoying going down as well as up, I can't go up without also going down, rising and falling are part of the same process, going down is as necessary in its way as going up, don't be discouraged by going down, falling is a prelude to rising, I must go on always, joyfully and freely.

See how these associations cluster around the idea of a swing and swinging. It is the swing that carries the message for the dreamer, telling him not to be discouraged by the inevitable setbacks to his progress in life. We can 'enjoy' – learn as much from – the setbacks as from the successes. If we learn from them in the right way, the former help us achieve the latter. Even in falling back there is security (the father's safe hands) provided we can see this always as part of life's lessons, the prelude to going forward once more.

In using amplification, don't fall into the trap of giving theory-based explanations (for example, 'a swing is probably a symbol for sexual intercourse') or of simply hunting for synonyms or stock expressions ('swing, cycle, swings and roundabouts, up and down, stop go, swing around, swing for it'). If you find yourself caught in this way, use the following techniques.

Say to yourself 'Let's imagine I'm talking to someone who has no idea what a swing is. Now let's describe it to them and give its appearance and its use and perhaps its history in a way that will leave them in no doubt as to what kind of thing it is.' Alternatively, ask yourself simply to describe some of your experiences with a swing, some of your memories, going back as far into the past as possible. One or other of these will usually serve to set off the flow of amplifications.

I asked in the last section why, if free association works so well, we need bother with alternative methods such as amplification. Let me now reword the question. If amplification works so well, why bother with free association? I've already said that free association is a good place for the beginner to start, because it helps open up the flow of creative, intuitive ideas so necessary in dreamwork, but there is more to it than this. No method of dream interpretation is perfect. Using only amplification, the dreamworker sometimes fails to make the intuitive leap between the symbol and its deeper levels of meaning. He or she becomes stuck, and needs to look at things from a new angle. Free association can provide this angle. Even if the free associations don't seem to lead you to your goal, the trail of images which they uncover is so rich that when you switch back to the original dream symbol again, new and more relevant amplifications spring into the mind, especially if you switch back suddenly, *now*.

Role playing. The third of the methods, adapted from that of Perls, we can best think of as role playing. Identify the significant things in your dreams or dream just as before, but take particular care not to neglect anything. Working with this method, almost everything you remember about the dream may be significant (the same can of course be true when working with free association or with amplification). The very fact that a particular dream object is occupying a humble position in the dream, or is *necessary to the dream action but hardly makes an appearance* – as for example the desk in a dream about sitting working in your office – may have something to tell you.

Once you have summoned up all the characters and events from the dream, see them as each in a sense representing a part of yourself. Take the role of each one in turn. What does it have to say to you? It's helpful to put two chairs facing each other, and move between them as you converse with these dream images. Working with the example given above – a dream about sitting in her office – a dreamworker talked with her desk in the following way:

DREAMWORKER: You're there every day. I sit at you from nine in the morning to five at night.

DESK: Yes, but you don't take much notice of me.

DREAMWORKER: Oh, I think I do. I notice you waiting for me in the morning. And I like to leave you tidy at night.

DESK: That's not noticing me. That's just using me. You don't even know who I am.

DREAMWORKER: All right, who are you then?

DESK: You can't do without me. If you didn't have me you wouldn't be able to work.

DREAMWORKER: That isn't answering my question.

DESK (*becoming suddenly angry*): Who are *you* to be asking questions? Why don't you look at yourself for a change?
DREAMWORKER: What would I see?
DESK: A mess. You tidy me because you can't tidy yourself. I'm the only thing that keeps you going. You put all sorts of things on top of me. And then you think that just because you tidy me up at the end of the day everything is all right..
DREAMWORKER: Okay. So I'm the part of me that gets all the credit for being good at my job, and you're the part that really carries everything.
DESK: Sure. And you'd better take more care of me, or one day I'll collapse under the weight of it all.

Further work showed the dreamer that the desk was part of her inner resources to which she wasn't giving enough time and attention. It was the part of her that supported her work and her home and her family, the dependable part of her on which everyone relied. It was there and it was solid, and it was indeed dependable, the most dependable thing in fact in the frantically busy 'mess' of her life. But it needed a little time to itself. In the words of the desk, it needed dusting and polishing occasionally, it needed to be admired, to have its scratches touched up, to be protected from hot coffee cups and typewriter correcting fluid. It didn't want less attention than the mechanical things like the telephone and the tape recorder which it had to support.

In work of this kind, there is a risk of over-dramatisation, of being carried away by the script instead of staying focused upon what the dream image is really trying to say. You become aware this is happening when the dialogue loses its emotional charge, and becomes simply wordy and clever. And the fact that you're taking the role of the dream image does mean that you shouldn't stray too far from it. As in Jungian dreamwork, constantly come back to the dream itself. For many people, role play is a highly effective way of getting into closer contact with the dream image, feeling it from the inside, so to speak, instead of only from the outside.

Important considerations at Level Two. In working at Level Two, look particularly for *wish fulfilments* when the dream shows you, usually in a disguised and exaggerated form, that there is repressed material or emotional drive in the unconscious which is seeking expression. And for *compensations*, when the dream makes up for some lack in the behaviour of your conscious self, and shows you your personality lacks the necessary wholeness and balance.

When working at Level Two with my own dreams or the dreams of others, my approach is to use the amplification method, and to slip into free association or into role play when it refuses to operate successfully or when a block is reached. So in the dream of the swing for example, the dreamer would if necessary either be told to let the mind start to 'free-wheel', or to shift into a different chair (or change his or her position on the floor) and start talking as the swing.

But sometimes dreams quite legitimately refuse to produce any Level Two material. This may be because they carry a straightforward Level One meaning which you've already identified. Or it may be because they're not particularly significant at any level. It's a mistake to think that dreams must *always* be fraught with meaning. Sometimes they seem to carry nothing more than trivia from the events of the day, and look very like the sort of rather inconsequential ponderings and imaginings we slip into in idle moments of waking life. Never try to force a dream to yield up some treasure or other. If there is something to yield up, it won't respond well to a forceful attack anyway, and if there isn't, you may simply end up inventing fictions, or becoming frustrated and giving up dreamwork altogether.

However, it *is* useful to ask why, from all the events that took place during the day, the dream chose to bring up one particular incident rather than another. The incident may look of no possible importance, but have a look at it all the same. The dream may have selected it for a purpose. So give it a chance to have its say, if only by pondering 'Why choose *that* of all things?' But if nothing emerges, and the dream carries no emotional charge of any kind, don't spend any longer on it. Dream interpretation is a great time-consumer, and it's better to save the attention you can give it for more profitable material.

Level Three Interpretation

Level Three dreams may impress themselves upon us by that

cosmic quality of which Jung speaks, but they may still need a lot of work before they reveal their full meaning. Unlike Level Two dreams, which may often use only symbols personal to the dreamer, Level Three dreams have a strong tendency to employ archetypal material (archetypes can operate at Level Two as well though, so their presence isn't an automatic indication you're now at Level Three). If you think you're working at Level Three, proceed as for Levels One and Two in your initial analysis of the dream content, but note particularly this archetypal material.

Once identified, don't assume the archetypes carry only their recognised archetypal meaning. Explore first any personal associations they may have, using free association, amplification or role play. Failure to do this may mean that you miss the message the archetype is trying to convey. For example, one woman dreamer dreamt that:

> I was being attacked by a savage dog, that first of all tried to bite me then began to call me names. I was rescued by a man who came out of the woods, and then the dog became friendly and started to lick my hand.

The dreamer's personal amplifications revealed a memory of having been frightened by a dog in a farmyard when she was young. This emphasised the child-like fears that were still part of her life. The archetypal figure of the talking dog which turns friendly then suggested to her that if she gives her hero side (her courageous side, symbolised by the archetypal hero figure who emerges from the concealment of the wood) a chance to reveal itself, it will tame the dog, which will then become her ally. The savage/tame dog then suggested to her the forceful, aggressive side of her nature, which she had always been fearful of using in case it consumed the gentler qualities which she felt were the only things about her that other people prized.

Had she avoided the initial personal association and begun immediately to relate to the dog as a wise animal which had something to tell her, she might have missed identifying what that something actually was. Similarly she might have missed it if she had focused immediately on the hero archetype.

But however you approach them, some Level Three dreams don't reveal their meaning all at once. The meaning only becomes clear as your life events unfold, perhaps over the following months, even the years. Don't be in too much of a hurry to grasp at this meaning. If you do, it could become hidden under a number of partial or even misleading interpretations. Instead, call the dream to mind from time to time, just like a memory from waking life. Recall its events in all the detail you can, including the feelings that they aroused. Go back to your dream diary to check these details, so that they don't become distorted, but at the same time don't 'fossilise' the dream. Regard its characters as living people, who may reappear in future dreams, and who are not bound just by the one adventure they shared with you. Illustrate the dream (as I advised on page 83) as soon as you can after it happened, and keep the illustration in your dream diary. Often this helps you recapture the flavour of the dream more fully than words on their own.

Dream Completion

Sometimes a dream remains maddeningly unfinished. It was just reaching a point where you felt something momentous was going to happen, and then it ended or you woke up. This can happen at all Levels, and with Level Three dreams you're left with a particular sense of loss. So resolve the dream for yourself. Put yourself as far as possible back into the atmosphere and the emotional feel of the dream, and let it play itself out. Again patience is the key, together with a determination not to let the rational mind (or wishful thinking!) take over. The first time you try this, often nothing happens. The dream remains static. Like the freeze frame in a video, the action and everybody in it remain where the dream left them.

Resolve to try again in the future. Sometimes the completion, like an interpretation, seems to be waiting for certain real life events to take place before it becomes clear. Sometimes it seems determined to remain forever enigmatic, not in order to be wilfully obscure but as a way of stimulating your creative thinking, of challenging you to go deeper and deeper into the unconscious.

Where you are able to complete a dream for yourself and the

ending has that indefinable sense of rightness about it, enter it
in your dream diary. But be sure to indicate in the diary that the
ending was arrived at in this way. And be open to the fact that
one day, out of the blue, a different ending may come to you.
This doesn't mean your original ending was wrong. It's more
likely a way of showing you that your life has moved on since
then, with the alternative endings giving you some idea of the
distance travelled.

Group Dreamwork

So far I've been assuming that, as with most people, you're
working on your dreams on your own. But if you have a group
of friends who share your interests in dreaming, you can work
together. Let me repeat the general warning though that any
interpretation arrived at must feel right to *you*. Don't accept the
interpretations of the rest of the group (or even of a therapist) if
they go against this feeling of 'rightness'. Suspect any
interpretation that fails to strike an emotional chord, either
positive or negative. Be honest and open with yourself, as with
all interpretations, but in the end make up your own mind on
whether they're appropriate or not.

I mention other people's interpretations because, human
nature being what it is, other people will try and offer their
opinions and solutions, no matter how hard they fight against
the temptation. But ideally, a dream group should simply listen
to your dream, and then help you with the process of exploring
it, and not offer you their solutions. For example, they can
suggest amplifications. They can even take the part of one of the
characters in a role play exercise if you're badly stuck. And they
can comment upon *your* amplifications and even upon your
interpretation ('Does that really seem right to you?', 'It sounds
as if you may be avoiding something there.', 'Could you take
the role of (one of your dream images)?', 'What about asking
that image what it means?').

Working with a group also gives you a chance to engage in a
more physical acting out of your dreams. I don't mean just role
play, I mean showing physically how you or the characters in
your dream actually behaved, or using postures to demonstrate

the emotions you felt during or after a dream. The rest of the group can then give amplifications or descriptions to these, and such contributions may help you to recognise elements about them that so far have eluded you.

In group work of this kind, it's vital that the atmosphere is supportive, accepting, and non-judgemental. No-one is there to make anyone else feel inadequate, or to laugh at their dreams, or to criticise their attempts at interpretation. Sharing dreams, especially emotional or deeply felt ones, is only possible in the right atmosphere. Anyone who can't recognise this has no place in the group until they can. Also out of place is someone who tries to monopolise proceedings, or to lay down the law as to what particular dream images mean (particularly if they brandish a dream dictionary in your face at the same time). Or anyone who is over-dogmatic about which approach to dream interpretation should be used. People who come together to share their dreams are courageous but this doesn't mean they're not vulnerable, and it's important that their vulnerability is respected if they are to make progress.

Using the Lessons of Dreams

Once you have begun to interpret your dreams, the question arises, what do you do with the lessons you learn? I can't pursue this too far, as it takes us away from dreams and into the whole vast and rich area of psychotherapy itself. The dream rarely tells you what to do; it shows you the path but not how to tread it. However by recognising the path, by identifying the problem, the solution in turn often becomes clear to us. The dream may show us we need to be more open to others, or more sensitive, or more assertive, or that we need to lay to rest the ghosts of the past. Having recognised this, the way ahead becomes clearer, provided we have the courage and the motivation to follow it.

But in using the lessons of dreams there are certain important guidelines to keep very much in mind:

* Don't be gullible. Dream interpretation is never an exact science. And dreams aren't always the fount of wisdom. Don't feel you must slavishly follow what the dream appears

to teach you if this goes against common sense. Don't
imagine the dream is always right and rational judgement
always wrong. Use dreams in the way you would use advice
from a knowledgeable friend. Sometimes the advice is good,
sometimes good but impractical, and sometimes it misses the
point.

* Attach more importance to advice gained from several
  dreams rather than from a single one (unless you're sure it's
  operating at Level Three).

* Keep monitoring your dreams. If you take advice from a
  dream, don't regard this as once and for all advice. Circumstances change, and the dream may well have something
  more to say on the subject a little later on.

* In spite of what I have to say about dream ESP in Chapter
  6, look to your dreams for advice on matters relating to how
  you should face up to your own complexes, how you should
  develop your potential, how you should better integrate your
  conscious and unconscious lives, how you should express
  and handle your emotions, how you should give rein to your
  creativity, rather than for advice on how you should make
  specific decisions or on how the future is going to turn out.

Let's now give some examples of how the things we've learnt
about dream interpretation and dream lessons can be applied to
specific types of dreams.

Nightmares and Bad Dreams

Most nightmares and bad dreams operate at both Level One
and Level Two. It's perfectly possible to have a dream just at
Level One about something unpleasant that has happened
during the day, but for the most part bad dreams involve both
a generalised Level One interpretation of how you see certain
aspects of the world, and a deeper Level Two interpretation
contained in the symbolism of the dream images themselves.

Nightmares take two obvious forms, dreams in which nasty
things are done to you, and dreams in which you do nasty things
to other people. We'll look at these in turn.

Nasty things done to you. The most frequently reported dreams of this kind involve being chased – either by a human or mythical creature – often with the accompanying sensation of being unable to run to safety. Other reports include being trapped, being in prison awaiting execution, being shot at or knifed, being sexually abused, blinded, choked or mutilated. Often there is an overpowering sense of evil, and the dreamer wakes with all the physical and emotional reactions that would be there if the events were happening in waking life. At a lesser but still unpleasant level there are dream experiences of being humiliated, scorned, or thrust into harrowing or stressful situations.

The first thing to emphasise about fearful dreams of this kind is that the fear lies in our reaction to them rather than in anything intrinsic to the dream itself. Odd as it may sound, the dream is still trying to be of use. The terrifying images it contains can be turned to our advantage if we know how – and can in the process be transformed, rather as the dog in the example on page 94 turned from savaging the dreamer to licking her hand.

How is this done? Think back to the Senoi practice in Chapter Two of rendering the dream harmless by facing the danger instead of running from it. But before you try this, your nightmare must be interpreted just like any other dream. Use free association or amplification or role play to find out what it's trying to tell you. Usually its message has to do (at Level One) with the recognition of fears that you are unable to understand and come to terms with, and (at Level Two) with the actual cause of these fears. Level Two interpretation often reveals these fears to be prompted by some quality in yourself that has been repressed, and which now needs integrating into your mature personality.

The quality may, for example, be self-assertion, or determination, or your will to succeed. Because of early experiences in the home or the school you were perhaps taught that these things were unacceptable (because inconvenient) to the adults in your life, with the result not only that you were unable to develop them, but also that you felt guilty and afraid at their very existence. You defended against this guilt by denying them, pretending they were not there. Now increasingly they are demanding recognition, a recognition which may be necessary for your further psychological development, but which reawakens your old fears about having something wild and imperfectly understood inside you.

An alternative possibility is that the dream represents some crisis or event in your life which you are afraid to face – something you need to master in order to express your personality more fully. Some task you have to perform, in connection for example with personal relationships or with your private or professional life.

Once you have identified the dream message, accepted the repressed quality in your personality and begun to integrate it into your conscious life, the nightmares will often cease of their own accord. Their purpose has been fulfilled. But if this doesn't happen, instruct your mind before going to sleep to turn and face your dream pursuer or stand up to your attackers or walk through the walls of your prison. Sometimes this succeeds in turning the dream into a lucid one (Chapter 7), but even if this is not the case the message usually gets through remarkably easily to the dreaming mind. And once the danger is confronted, most people report that who or whatever was causing it becomes friendly or turns away or disappears.

If this method is used in conjunction with dream interpretation, the dream has fulfilled its purpose and given you its message. And you may find that dreams now come which are a friendly, non-frightening development of the nightmare. The nightmare dream characters or situations are transformed into allies, and interpretation of these new dreams may reveal further messages to you from your unconscious on the same theme but in a friendly form and coming from an even deeper level.

Facing your fear in a dream may also help you to be less fearful in waking life. I referred to this possibility in Chapter 2, and many people spontaneously report that this happens (gains in self-confidence are also reported). And since dream emotions are physiologically every bit as real as waking emotions, there's no good psychological reason why it shouldn't.

Nasty things done to somebody else. Dreams in which you are doing unpleasant things to other people can be carrying the same message. Some aspect of yourself that needs expressing is currently being repressed, with the result (Level One interpretation) that you feel a great deal of undirected anger and frustration. Don't be worried that, as the dream is a violent one, this aspect must be to do with violence. The dream violence is usually to do with the strength of the frustration which this repressed part of you feels, rather than with its actual nature. Level Two interpretation may reveal this repressed part as nothing more than your creativity, or your individuality, or your desire to make a mark on the world.

In my experience, dreams of this kind also represent in some people a high level of free-floating anxiety. That is, the anxiety where we feel worried, depressed and ill-at-ease, or vaguely guilty and unhappy about ourselves, but without knowing quite why. The unconscious is prone to dramatise this anxiety for us along the lines of 'Okay, I'm worried about something; what could it be? what's the *worst* possible thing I could be worried about? killing someone? must be that; okay, let's act it out.' The acting out is thus an attempt by the unconscious to bring the anxiety to the surface and release it. The only problem is that with free-floating anxiety there isn't anything specific we're worrying about. It's an anxiety habit, either short term or long, into which we've slipped as a result of previous life experiences.

Although the dream hasn't got the details of the message right, it has still performed a useful function. It's brought to the dreamer's attention the destructive effect of free-floating anxiety or of feelings of guilt, prompting him or her to let them go and to use the emotional and mental energy involved more productively.

Dreams in which nasty things are done to others but in which you are the observer rather than the actor seem for many people to fall into the same category. Again interpretation shows that the mind is often preoccupied by fear of catastrophe, but of a nameless, unspecified kind. The dream dramatises a justification for this fear, thus allowing some of the emotion involved to be released, and brings to the attention of the waking mind the extent to which this fear is dominating and distorting your view of reality.

Embarrassing Dreams

Though not as bad as nightmares, embarrassing dreams (often recurring ones), in which the dreamer is asked to make a speech or sit an examination for which they haven't prepared, or suddenly finds him or herself naked in public, often cause people great distress. The Level One interpretation is usually clear. The dreamer, although perhaps highly successful in waking life, nevertheless feels vulnerable and exposed. If we're honest, we're none of us as sure of ourselves as we seem. Even if the world sees us as an expert, we're appalled sometimes by our lack of knowledge ('surely there *must* be people who know more about the subject than me!') and frightened that we will prove inadequate, or that our ignorance will be exposed, or that our hard-won success will suddenly be taken from us.

Level Two interpretation will help us identify the source of this vulnerability. Perhaps parents who always expected too much from us as children. Perhaps traumatic experiences (again often in childhood) when our inexpertise or our lack of knowledge about something was cruelly exposed. Once the source is identified, the dreams will often stop of their own accord.

Though public nakedness is often only a symbol of this general vulnerability, for some people dream interpretation traces it back to an over-prudish upbringing in which the human body was regarded as sinful, and the child's natural curiosity about his or her own and other people's bodies was insensitively punished and suppressed. Interpretation can also sometimes reveal feelings of sexual inadequacy, but this is not especially common. In addition to working on the interpretation of their public nakedness in dreams, I advise people (rather like facing their fears in a nightmare) actually to enjoy the nakedness. Where there is a link with punishment and guilt as a result of adult disapproval years ago of the dreamer's natural tendency to childhood exhibitionism, this switch from embarrassment to enjoyment helps release the repressed emotions. Subsequently, the nudity dreams may stop (rather to the dreamer's disappointment!).

One of the main lessons to be learnt from dream interpretation

– or rather one of the benefits that arises from this interpretation – doesn't come from the specific advice dreams are able to give. It comes from the fact that through dreamwork you become more attuned over a period of time to your creative, intuitive self. Dreamwork leaves you feeling more whole, more open to your emotions, often gentler and more understanding of yourself and others. It can help men feel more in contact with the feminine side of their natures, and women more in contact with the masculine in theirs. Dreamwork gives you a deeper sense of yourself, a realisation that much of your life takes place below the surface of your consciousness, that to live only in our rational, logical thoughts is to skate thinly over the waters of our being.

Dreamwork is free, open and readily available. It represents not an escape from reality but a movement into a wider, richer, more comprehensive reality. It asks little from us but time, patience, and the use of a few relatively simple techniques. And it repays us a thousand times over. Now let's look at other areas of being where dreamwork may have a part to play, beginning with dreams and ESP.

6

ESP IN DREAMS

Many scientists still refuse to accept the existence of ESP (extra sensory perception). In summary their arguments are firstly that it hasn't yet been demonstrated under properly controlled conditions, and secondly that even if it had they would still have to disbelieve it as it goes so comprehensively against the laws of nature.

The answer to the first of these arguments is 'look at the evidence'. If one chooses to ignore the eye-witness accounts of spontaneous ESP (the sighting of ghosts, the awareness for example of other people's unspoken thoughts, the occurrence of long-odds coincidences, premonitions about the future) on the grounds that witnesses may be naive or lying, we still have to explain away the formidable results produced in laboratory experiments every bit as carefully conducted as those in other branches of scientific enquiry. Produced moreover not only by parapsychologists who specialise in investigations into the paranormal (and who might be accused of having a vested interest in proving its existence) but by reputable physicists and psychologists who actively risk lowering their reputation in the eyes of their colleagues by even admitting to an interest in the subject.

This evidence is well documented, and unless one uses the argument of massive incompetence or massive fraud on the part of the scientists involved (an argument even less credible than the existence of ESP itself), it shows that ESP can be demonstrated in the form of telepathy (the direct communication of impressions from one mind to another), clairvoyance (the acquisition of information paranormally and without its being first in the mind of another person), precognition (knowledge of some future event which cannot be inferred from present data) and psychokinesis (the paranormal movement of objects).

Similarities Between ESP and Dreams

As with creativity and dreams, there are many points of resemblance between the experiences people apparently have in ESP and the experiences they have in dreams. Let's take ESP experiences first. When impressions are received telepathically or clairvoyantly or precognitively they are notoriously vague and often symbolic. They appear to impinge initially upon the unconscious and have to be conveyed from there into consciousness. They get the details wrong. They mix up apparently unconnected people and events. They behave creatively, often elaborating misleadingly on the information they set out to convey. And they stubbornly remain outside the range of our conscious control.

To each of these characteristics one can add 'and so do dreams'. It's not surprising, therefore, that listening to someone describing their ESP impressions is very like listening to someone describing their dream or hypnogogic images. There is the same account of fleeting impressions. The same professed bewilderment as to what these impressions are trying to convey. The same insistence that they leap into the mind from some unrecognised source. The same confession of difficulty in holding on to them or in prompting them to elaborate on themselves.

ESP in Dreams

In view of these similarities, it is not surprising that people have maintained from ancient times that dreams can carry ESP messages. As we saw in Chapter 2, the Egyptians and the Greeks thought that the gods spoke to them in dreams, while both the Old and the New Testaments have God speaking to man in the same way. In modern times, the literature on ESP is full of examples of apparent ESP in dreams. One of the earliest is from the monumental survey of ghosts and apparitions carried out for the newly-formed Society for Psychical Research by Gurney, Myers and Podomore in 1886. The dreamer tells how she was woken in the early morning:

> feeling that I had had a hard blow on my mouth and with a distinct sense that I had been cut and was bleeding from under my upper lip...I was astonished not to see any blood, and only then realised it was impossible anything could have struck me, as I lay fast asleep in bed, and so I thought it was only a dream.

The dreamer tells us that later, at breakfast, she noticed that her husband, who had been out on an early morning sailing trip, was dabbing at his lip with his pocket handkerchief.

> I said 'Arthur, why are you doing that?...I know that you've hurt yourself, but I'll tell you why afterwards.' He said, 'Well, when I was sailing, a sudden squall came, throwing the tiller suddenly round, and it struck me a bad blow in the mouth under the upper lip, and it has been bleeding a good deal and won't stop.'

Another dream involving personal injury, this time to an animal, was reported by the novelist Rider Haggard in 1904. Half waking from a nightmare, Haggard had a distinct impression of his retriever dog, Bob, lying on his side among brushwood by a river... 'In my vision the dog was trying to speak to me in words and, failing, transmitted to my mind in an undefined fashion the knowledge that it was dying.'

When the following morning it was discovered Bob was not in his usual place in the yard, a search was mounted and his dead body was eventually discovered in a nearby river. The testimony of some railway workers, together with a vet's report on the body, indicated that the dog had probably been struck by a train while crossing a railway bridge, and had fallen from there into the water at or a little before the time of Haggard's dream.

Disaster is the subject of both these dreams, and disaster – usually involving people or animals or objects dear to the dreamer – crops up frequently in accounts of dream ESP. These disaster dreams are particularly impressive when they occur spontaneously, without the dreamer having any prior knowledge that illness or danger threatens the people or things concerned. But rather than take up space by giving more examples from the many others available, it's more useful to ask whether ESP in dreams occurs only on rare momentous occasions such as these, or whether it happens frequently but is only noticed or remembered when something especially significant makes it stick in our mind.

In Search of Paranormal Dreams

One of the most interesting attempts to answer this question was made by J. W. Dunne over a period of more than 20 years earlier this century. Dunne's great interest in dreams was sparked off by a particularly impressive disaster dream, though it happened not to people he knew but to the inhabitants of an island hundreds of kilometres away. Dunne had already had two or three dreams in which he seemed to gain knowledge of future events; then one night while living in South Africa he dreamt he was standing on an island, 'an island of which I had dreamed before – an island which was in imminent peril from a volcano. And when I saw the vapour spouting from the ground, I gasped: "It's the island! Good Lord, the whole thing is going to *blow up!*" ' In the dream Dunne then tried to warn the *French* (he was sure they were French) authorities that the volcano was about to explode and that *4,000* lives were at risk.

When the next batch of newspapers arrived from Britain a few days later, Dunne found a prominent account of the eruption of Mont Pelee on the French island of Martinique, with the 'probable loss of over 40,000 lives'. Thus his dream was correct in both the details of the eruption and in the fact that the island concerned was French. The dream had however substituted 4,000 lives for 40,000, but when reading the newspaper account Dunne did in fact misread '40,000 lives' as '4,000', and it was not until much later that he realised his mistake. This suggested to him that his dream obtained its precognitive information not from the actual events on Martinique themselves but from the misread newspaper article, and that it had then dramatised these events for him.

This dream was followed by a number of other clearly precognitive ones over the next few years. Space allows only one example. Whilst on holiday in Austria, Dunne dreamt he was walking along a fenced-off pathway between two fields when he noticed a horse behaving in an alarming way in the field to his left. After reassuring himself the horse couldn't escape from the field he continued his journey, only to hear a moment later hooves thundering after him. Realising the horse had after all got out of the field, he ran towards a flight of wooden steps further down the path, and was trying his best to reach them when he awoke.

The following day, while on a fishing trip with his brother, Dunne heard the latter call 'Look at that horse!'. Glancing across the river, Dunne saw the scene of his dream. Everything was on a smaller scale, but the essentials were correct. There was the fenced-off pathway between two fields, there were the wooden steps at the end of the pathway, and there was the horse behaving in the same over-excited way.

Dunne then related his dream to his brother, and was just saying 'at any rate *this* horse can't get out' when the horse succeeded in doing just that, and began thundering down the path towards the wooden steps. The dream had ended at this point, but in real life the horse swerved round the steps, plunged into the river and swam towards Dunne and his brother, who beat a hasty retreat. Brought to its senses by the cold water, however, the animal merely looked at the brothers as it emerged from the river, and then snorted and trotted off down the road.

As a result of his dreams, Dunne developed an intricate theory of time, in which he saw dream images as portraying scenes from both our past and our future experiences. To the dreaming mind, past and future are much the same, and it is thus free to wander between them at will, often ranging many years backwards or forwards, and sometimes combining both past and future events in the same dream. Looking for further evidence in support of his theory, Dunne kept a careful record of his dreams, studying them for signs of any connection with past and future events. He was a curiously modern figure, in that many years before the time when dream research established that we probably all dream every night, he was convinced that 'dreamless sleep is an illusion of memory'. What happens is that one 'forgets the dreams at the very instant of waking'.

So the fact that at the start of his research he only remembered a dream one night in every ten, was no deterrent to him. By experimenting, he found that 'the dodge for recalling the forgotten dreams is quite simple'. Dunne's dodge is much the same as the technique given in Chapter 1, but it is worth repeating because it is the essence of work of this kind. Dunne says that 'A notebook and pencil are kept under the pillow, and, *immediately* on waking, before you even open your eyes, you set yourself to remember the rapidly vanishing dream.' Hang on to the single incident that is probably all you can recall, and try to remember the details. Don't make a conscious effort to remember anything more. Like a flash, a section of the dream in which that incident occured will come back to you...more important...with that section there usually comes...an isolated incident from a previous dream. Get hold of as many of these incidents as you can...then jot [them down] as briefly as possible in your notebook.' If you have difficulty in remembering even a single dream incident upon awaking, focus instead upon whatever it is you are thinking about, and then try to recall *why* you are thinking about it. This usually unlocks the dream memory.

You then concentrate on each incident in turn, writing down the details that come into mind in connection with it, and then search for resemblances between these details and actual happenings in the days before or after the dreams. Dunne cautions that we must look closely for these resemblances. They are like 'trying to read a book while looking out for words which might mean something spelled backwards'. Particularly in the case of the future, we are all too ready to pass over or reject them, and for this reason it is as well to play a psychological trick upon ourselves and pretend that the dreams happened after and not before the future events concerned. But if one very trivial (no matter how trivial) similarity between dream events and real-life events is noticed, the dream can then be reread and the corroborative details allowed to 'come slowly and singly to light'.

Dunne suggests experimenting on remembering your

dreams and seeing similarities between them and past and future events at times (holiday times for example) when you are free from the monotony of everyday life. Again he gives many examples of how his recorded dreams showed fragments of things to come. Here is just one.

During the day, Dunne was out shooting when he found himself on land where he realised he might have no right to be. Two men started shouting at him from different directions, and appeared to be urging on a furiously barking dog. The shouting and barking came nearer, and Dunne turned tail and escaped through a gate before his pursuers came in sight. On reading his dream diary that evening he came across a dream incident recorded some two weeks earlier. 'Hunted by two men and a dog.' Not only could he not remember the dream, he could not even remember writing it down, though it had been recorded so recently.

Dunne persuaded friends and relatives to try out his methods, with every sign of success. For example, immediately upon her arrival at a country hotel a cousin was told of a woman guest whom everyone suspected of being German (the date was 1918). Later the cousin met the woman in the hotel gardens (which in extent and character resembled a public park) and found her dressed in a black skirt with a black-and-white striped blouse and her hair scraped back in a bun. In a dream recorded and lodged with Dunne two days *before* this meeting, the cousin had dreamt of meeting in a public garden a German woman whom she suspected of being a spy, and who was dressed in just this way and with the same hair style.

This evidence was produced only eight days after the cousin first started using Dunne's methods. Before doing so she rarely remembered her dreams and was positive she had never had precognitive experiences of any kind.

Dreaming Race Winners

It is sometimes argued that if ESP in dreams really happens we would be dreaming useful things like Derby winners. Those who advance this argument usually do so as a kind of 'proof' that ESP doesn't exist. But there are, in fact, a number of instances of people who claim to have won money on horses as a result of precognitive dreams (let's call them tipster dreams). One of the most impressive series of such dreams was reported in the late 1950s by Harold Horwood, a chartered electrical engineer and an ex-senior civil servant. His case merits examination in some detail.

Horwood reports he developed his ability to 'dream true' as an incidental result of intensive meditation practices. In his first tipster dream he saw a telegram with the words 'The name of the winner of the big race is, yes, it hasn't got one.' He dismissed this as nonsense, only to find the winner of the Cambridgeshire the next day was *Esquire* at odds of 40/1. Sufficiently intrigued, he decided to take more notice of any similar dream in the future. Six months later, on the eve of the Oaks, he dreamt three names, but the following morning could remember only the first two of them, *Goodwin Sands* and *Steady Aim*. *Goodwin Sands* was not in the list of runners (though a horse of this name won a minor race a few days later), so Horwood backed *Steady Aim* for a place. It won at 7/1.

Five months later he was woken by a shout which sounded like *Sehoney*. On investigation he found a horse called *Sayani* entered for the Cambridgeshire due to be run four weeks later, and backed it to win at the ante-post price of 40/1. It did so in a field of 34 runners.

Ten days before the next big race, the Manchester November Handicap, Horwood dreamt the name *Las Vegas*, and backed it to win at 20/1. It came home first of the 23 runners.

After a lull in his dreaming, which he attributed to going back on his private promise to use his winnings only for non-selfish purposes (and during which efforts to force matters were unsuccessful), Horwood returned to winning ways when he found that if he awoke in pitch darkness and opened his eyes immediately, he would sometimes see for a fleeting moment the name of a horse. But he also began to experience symbolic pictorial dreams, as when he dreamt one night of a single female lion amongst males and *Lions Lass* turned out to be the winner the following day.

On occasions the dream altered the winner's name somewhat, as when Horwood dreamt of *Mallory Marshes* and the winner turned out to be *Marshmallow*. At other times the information was cryptic, as when he dreamt 'The first shall be fourth' on the eve of the Grand National, and found the following day that the favourite, *Cromwell*, did in fact come home fourth.

Horwood was by no means always successful, but his successes were considerably more spectacular than his failures, and on his own estimate he won £100 for every £10 lost. During 1958 alone he claimed to dream more than 20 winners, including the Queen's horse *Pall Mall* which won the 2,000 guineas. Bookmakers' statements showing his major successes were lodged by way of proof with his printers and with a national newspaper.

When Horwood did fail, this seemed most often to be due to faulty interpretation of the symbolism in a pictorial dream, or to attempts by the rational waking mind to interfere with the information given by the dream. Over the course of time he also found that his dream indications became more tricky, more symbolic and harder to interpret. He discovered that one way of dealing with this was to divide the names of the runners in a big race into two or more separate lists, and allow the dream to indicate (symbolically or directly) which of the lists contained the winner's name and what position in the list it occupied.

Members of Horwood's family also seemed to have some success in dreaming true. Briefly his advice to others boils down to the fact that, after the usual practice of keeping a notepad beside the bed and writing down your dreams at the moment of waking, you should go through the following steps:

1. Have faith in your ability to dream true.
2. Decide on a race about a week ahead.
3. Divide the runners up at random into two lists, and give each runner a number.
4. Read through the lists each night before going to sleep, without trying to memorise them but saying to yourself (out loud if you like) 'I want to know which one is going to win.'
5. On waking, make brief notes of your dreams, *no matter how apparently irrelevant*.
6. Study this dream material for clues such as initials, number of letters, first or second list, position in list, and so on.

7. Repeat the exercise each night before the race, altering the position of the runners within and between the two lists in the hope that you will be able to use the clues to narrow down onto one horse.
8. Don't be discouraged.

My own rooted dislike for both horse racing and for gambling has prevented me from putting Horwood's system to the test. But it can of course be tried as a research exercise in an effort to pick the winner of the FA cup or of the world snooker championship or of any other sporting contest. If you do this, be sure though not to let the rational mind intrude too much in interpreting your 'clues'. Remember that the dreaming mind and the rational mind are working at two different levels.

In Horwood's case, it's relevant to ask why, if his unconscious knew the winner, it chose to operate at what appears to be a strange amalgam of Levels One and Two rather than simply at Level One. This looks strongly like another example of the phenomenon we talked about in Chapter 3, namely the dream's intention to set a puzzle, to start the conscious mind thinking, to surprise the waking mind out of its over-reliance on the rational, analytical approach.

Take for example Horwood's first tipster dream, 'The name of the winner of the big race is, yes, it hasn't got one.' *Esquire* of course isn't a name but a title, so the clue is an accurate and (relevant to my discussion of dream intelligence in Chapter 3) an intelligent one. Looked at more closely, there is also an intriguing suggestion that the dream was about to give the answer in a direct form – the 'yes' in the clue sounds very like the beginning of the word *Esquire* – then changed its mind and substituted a brainteaser instead.

There are a number of occasions when the dream seems to want not only to puzzle but to be mischievously playful. For example it would alter names, as when *Marshmallow* becomes *Mallory Marshes*. And there was one memorable occasion when Horwood awoke saying to himself 'Can't tell you', and then found *Cantelo* was one of the runners on his list. He backed it successfully to win, but the dream seemed to be teasing him into taking the clue at face value, and jumping to the conclusion that it had nothing useful to tell him. It told him the name of the winner, but it gave it to him in a form which could so easily have led him to conclude the dream was unable to provide him with a clue of any kind.

From these and from many of the other examples in Horwood's book, one is left with the impression that it was not only his ability to dream true which was important, but also the meticulous and patient way in which he set about interpreting the information his dreams provided. In fact, Horwood gives only one single instance of a dream actually presenting him with a name in its correct form (*Tulyar*), and one is left to speculate on the number of people who may have dreamt the winners of big races without realising it.

Other Tipster Dreams

Although the further examples I'm going to give of tipster dreams all operate at Level One, this shouldn't be taken as indicating that Level Two tipster dreams of the type experienced by Horwood are in a minority. What it probably shows is that few people think of searching Level Two dreams for tips, while they're ready to act when tips are given – probably much more rarely – at Level One. The first examples are from the well-known voyager into the outer fringes of science, Thelma Moss. Moss tells of her research with a woman, an educational psychologist, who dreamt the winners of races three or four times a week over a period of four months. Up until the time in fact when her husband used the winnings to buy a car, whereupon the dreams stopped abruptly. (The similar lull in Horwood's dreaming when he broke his promise to use his winnings only for non-selfish purposes is further proof of my argument on page 28 of the moral abilities of the dreaming mind.)

Moss's subject reported that her dreams were vivid and were actually of the races themselves, with the winners' names announced loud and clear over the public address system. She confessed to having no interest at all in racing, and never to have heard of the names of the winning horses prior to her dreams. Another case researched by Moss was of a woman who dreamt the *number* of a winning horse. Refusing to gamble for religious reasons she did nothing about her dream, but on subsequently dreaming a winning double she decided to back it to make money for charity. Both horses in the double won at long odds.

The third example given by Moss is of a television producer who dreamt the names of the first three horses in an unspecified race. After some searching he found a race in which all three of these horses were running, and won a considerable sum of money on the winner. Interestingly, he told several witnesses about the dream *before* the race actually took place, which adds considerably to the scientific value of his experience.

To name just three further examples. Colin Wilson some years ago reported the case of the peer Lord Kilbracken who dreamt and subsequently backed a number of winners during his student days, again in some cases confiding in independent witnesses before the races took place. Also some years ago the televison science correspondent Michael Fairlie, though not a racing or gambling man, reported dreaming several winners over a period of time – a brave and valuable admission for a man in his position. Dream researchers Ullman and Zimmerman provide the third example: a correspondent of theirs who dreamt the numbers of the first two horses on each of three consecutive nights, and later dreamt the numbers of two further doubles.

Recording Your Precognitive Dreams

Before you try looking for tipster dreams, study your dream diary as did Dunne for any dreams which seem to relate to the events of the following day. In my own case, I have amassed a number of these. The majority relate to relatively trivial things, just as the dream often seems to pick up trivial events from the previous day and to weave these into its picture show. Here are a few examples of these dreams, all of which occurred over a comparatively short period of time.

In the dream I met a friend of mine called Terry, who I had not seen for some time. He looked so thin that I wondered if he had been ill. A few days later in waking life, I met his wife who I had also not seen for some time. She immediately greeted me with the words 'You wouldn't recognise Terry, he's so slim!'

Further conversation revealed that Terry had been dieting. Though of a muscular build, it had never occurred to me to think of Terry as overweight, and the topic of weight or of dieting has never entered into any of the conversations I have had with him.

In the dream I dropped a small hard object which I couldn't identify but which I thought might be some kind of shelf ornament, on my right foot. The following morning, getting a small vitamin bottle from a shelf in the cupboard, I dropped it on the very same spot on top of my right foot (the only time I can ever remember such a thing happening).

In the dream I heard church bells and told someone it was possible to protest against them if they disturb you. In next morning's paper I read of a vicar who was to protest against the amplified calls to prayer from a mosque because he found them disturbing.

I dreamt of a garden in which strangely and incongruously there were a number of stationary railway box cars. Next morning on reading (for the first time) some details of Vivekananda's life I came upon the news that he had spent his first night in the USA in a railway box car.

I apologise for including the next dream, but since both dream and waking event refer to such a bizarre and unlikely happening it's worth a mention. The dream was a mildly erotic one in which I dreamt of someone telling me she found my penis a sexual turn-off because it was twisted (a gross libel on the truth I hasten to add). Next morning in the paper I read of an unfortunate man who was sueing for damages because a circumcision operation had left his penis twisted, with adverse affects on his sex life.

With all these examples, it could be argued that since we dream so many things every night, and since so many things happen the following day, then by the law of averages there are bound occasionally to be some similarities between the two sets of events on the grounds of chance alone. This is no doubt true. But one of the most noticeable things about similarity dreams, such as the examples I've just given, is that the link between the dream and the real-life event usually hits one with particular force. Often in fact one has no memory of the dream until the real-life event takes place, whereupon it leaps vividly into the memory.

And as in my last example, often the two things focus upon something so unusual that to put it all down to chance stretches credulity. If the dream featured routine events, the sort of things that happen often in waking life, then coincidence would be the obvious explanation. But in my own dream records, I find few instances of synchronicity involving mundane matters of this kind. Just as with dreams which contain snippets of events from the past, dreams which apparently pick up events from the future prefer to focus upon the odd, often rather quirky happenings. In themselves these happenings may be of little consequence, yet they are just the kind of things that catch the eye, and just the kind of thing that dreams seem to like to weave into their fabric.

It's also noticeable that the way in which the dream treats the waking event to which it seems to refer is similar whether this event is a past or a future one. In both cases the dream distorts, elaborates, gets details subtly wrong. No dream theory (even the forgetting theory) disputes the fact that dreams are often connected to past events, so a recognition of this pattern, while it doesn't prove dreams can operate precognitively, alerts us to the things for which we should look when examining our dream diaries for possible precognitive incidents.

Laboratory Research Into Dream ESP

Apart from the two examples I gave at the beginning of this chapter, I've concentrated upon allegedly precognitive dreams when discussing dream ESP. But some of the best evidence so far gathered in the laboratory for dream ESP has to do not with precognition but with telepathy. One of the most widely used laboratory techniques is for an experimenter to monitor a volunteer's sleep over a period of seven or eight nights and, each time he or she enters REM sleep, to alert a third person in another room (known as the sender) who then concentrates on a randomly selected picture, the contents of which are unknown to both the experimenter and the dreamer. At the end of each REM period, the dreamer is awakened and asked to report his or her dream.

At the conclusion of the seven or eight night experimental

period, a panel of independent judges is given the target pictures together with the tape recorded dream reports, but with no clues as to which picture was being 'sent' when each of the dreams took place. The judges are simply asked to say which picture (if any) relates in their opinion to which dream. The hypothesis being that if ESP is operating, there will be a more frequent match between pictures and dreams than would be expected on the grounds of chance alone.

At the Maimonides Medical Centre in New York, where much of the work of this kind has been carried out, Krippner and Ullman report a significant degree of successful matching. In one of their experiments, carried out over eight nights and involving 64 possible combinations between pictures and dreams, results showed that pictures and dreams matched each other with a frequency that would be expected to happen by chance only once in a thousand times.

BOX 9
DEVELOPING DREAM ESP

The guidelines provided by Dunne, by Horwood and by the experimental work of Krippner and Ullman and summarised in the text, are a good place to start the business of exploring your own dreams for ESP. The evidence provided by these authorities suggests that this exploration is also effective in developing your ESP. As with much dream work, the very fact of beginning to take notice of what is happening within your dreams seems to be instrumental in increasing their scope and richness.

If you haven't the facilities for setting up the sort of experiment used by Krippner and Ullman, you can try something simpler. Ask a friend to set you a puzzle, the answer to which you can't get by normal means. For example he or she may hide one of your personal possessions (it should be something of which you're fond and which you very much want to recover) in an unlikely place, or simply draw a picture or write a piece of information on a piece of paper and seal it in an envelope which is then locked away in a drawer. As you drift off to sleep each night, hold the puzzle in your mind and ask the dream to provide you with the solution. Do this for several nights, and don't be impatient.

One possible difficulty is that the dream may provide the answer during your early phase of dreaming, and dreams from

BOX 9
DEVELOPING DREAM ESP

this phase are unlikely to be remembered in the morning. Try and counter this tendency by thinking about the puzzle from time to time during the day, so that the message that you want the answer is firmly lodged in your unconscious.

Synchronous Dreams
Another approach is to try with a friend to experience the same dreams. For example, agree to meet with your friend in a certain place in the dream. There are a number of published accounts of success with this technique, though in the maddening way of dreams you may find it works for you on the first night and then doesn't happen again for weeks.

Dreams of this kind may not necessarily provide possible evidence of ESP. This evidence only emerges if you find that you and your friend had similar experiences in the dream, or said things to each other which both of you recall in the same way the following morning. It's important for you both to write down your dreams with all possible details *before* you start to discuss them with each other. It's all too easy to start imagining you remember things once you start hearing them from your friend.

Dream Psychometry
Another interesting possibility which appears to produce results for some people is to try to gain information about an object (psychometrise it) of which you know nothing. Hold the object in your hands before going to sleep, then keep the idea of it in your thoughts as you go off to sleep. You can try the same technique with the photo of someone unknown to you. Some people find it helps to place the object or the photo under their pillows. In the morning, record your dreams, no matter how irrelevant, then study them for meaning in the usual way.

As one would expect, the dreams gave an impressionistic, symbolic version of the actual target picture. For example, when the target was the well-known Japanese painting 'Downpour at Shono', the subject reported dreaming 'something about an Oriental man who was ill...A fountain...a water spray that would shoot up...Walking with someone on the street...It was raining and it was night and it had a sort of heavy feeling.'

The correspondence was sufficiently close for the judges to

match the picture with the dream, but notice how the stooping posture of the Oriental man is misinterpreted as illness, while the fierce quality of the rain is represented as 'a fountain', 'a water spray', and the bad weather as 'a heavy feeling'.

Provided you have two co-operative friends and you're prepared to be awoken after each bout of REM sleep for a night or two, this is not a difficult experiment to try for yourself. In the absence of monitoring equipment, REM sleep is detectable by the restlessness of the subject and by the visible rolling of his or her eyeballs behind the eyes.

Conclusion

Except for laboratory work of this kind, it is very difficult to establish beyond question the existence of ESP in dreams. But the apparent similarity between ESP experiences and dream experiences, together with the persistent reports throughout history of precognitive, telepathic and clairvoyant messages obtained while dreaming, must lead us to take seriously the idea of a link between the two. The implications of such a link are profound, not just for our understanding of dreaming but also for our understanding of the human mind and of the nature of reality itself.

7

LUCID DREAMING

It's time now to discuss a strange but widely reported phenomenon, the apparent ability of spiritually advanced men and women to remain conscious throughout the hours of sleep. Until we've experienced such a condition for ourselves we can't really know what it means, but accounts available to us suggest they inhabit a night-long dream world in which they are *aware* that they're dreaming, and able as a result to control the dream state and use it for spiritual growth, or for gaining information not available by normal means (dream ESP again).

It is said that, either in the dream state or in out-of-the-body experiences (of which more shortly), they are also able to project themselves to those who need them – their students, the sick, the unhappy. People who claim first-hand knowledge of these states tell me that after such visits both visitor and visited are often able the following morning to recount in the same kind of detail what actually happened (see also the technique referred to in Box 9, though here the dreaming only takes place at the usual unconscious level).

Without aspiring to such feats, it is possible for most (probably all) of us to retain or regain consciousness during at least some of our dreams. That is, to observe and control with our conscious minds the dream material served up by the unconscious. Dreams in which this conscious control operates are usually referred to as *lucid dreams*, and their characteristic is that when experiencing them one actually knows one is asleep and dreaming. Lucid dreams have a particular quality to them which, once experienced, is not easily forgotten. The quality commences the moment when, in the middle of a dream, the realisation dawns that 'Ah, I must be dreaming!' Most people, myself included, find that, at this moment, the dream seems instantly to open out. Colours become more vivid, more vibrant. People and events, though one is now aware they are only part of a dream, seem paradoxically to become more real. And – this is the key element – the dreamer knows that the dream can be controlled. He or she can usually decide what to do and where to go. (I say 'usually' because it doesn't always work that way; in a lucid dream there is always an element of the unexpected; the final decisions are still in the hands of the dream itself.)

Often it remains hard to hang on to this state. Sometimes one wakes. Sometimes the dream slips back into an ordinary dream. Sometimes it remains only intermittently lucid. Maddeningly, having had one lucid dream, the dreamer may have to wait weeks, months, perhaps years before experiencing another. On occasions, several lucid dreams may come together over a very short period, followed by a long fallow interval during which nothing happens. There seems no rhyme nor reason about it. One tries a technique for lucid dreaming, and Eureka it works – perhaps for several nights running – then for no apparent reason it ceases to work, and one seems to be back where one started.

There are no accurate figures for the number of people who regularly dream lucidly, although such evidence as we have suggests around 70 per cent of people claim to have had lucid dreams at some time or other. This is quite a high figure, and raises questions as to whether the people surveyed fully understand what lucid dreams are. For example, some people claim to me that most of their dreams are lucid, but further questioning shows they have only a sketchy idea of what the term means. In a lucid dream, the dreamer has much more than a shadowy, fleeting awareness that a dream is taking place. He or she is able to hold onto and expand that awareness so that something approaching normal waking consciousness is achieved. Once this happens it is possible to view the dream with the kind of awareness one watches a film or the TV – except that now one is not a spectator but part of the action.

The Strange Quality of Lucid Dreams

And part of the action in a very strange way. For – and it is this that gives the impression that in lucid dreams one really is travelling in another world as objectively 'real' as this one – although one's mind is conscious and able to take decisions, the dream scenery and often the dream events are still sketched in for one by the secret, mysterious processes of the unconscious.

So if I decide in a lucid dream to visit a South Sea Island for example, I don't have to recall what such an island looks like, and then try and imagine it. The island is created for me, and turns out to be as full of surprises as a real place visited for the first time. It isn't even a clever amalgam of my past experiences, a set of permutations from my memory banks. It has all the appearance of a real place created not by my mind but by the hand of nature herself.

Even if I visit a familiar place in the dream, I don't have to construct the details consciously. The dream will do the constructing for me, down to the last detail, but with those subtle differences from waking life that are characteristic of non-lucid dreams. I may find two windows in a room where only one should exist, a door in a wall where in real life there is no door, a friend who looks older or younger, taller or shorter than they should. And no matter how striking these differences are to me, I may be unable to change them to fit the real facts of the matter.

Van Eeden, one of the most meticulous chroniclers of lucid dreams, had the distinct impression that the world he experienced during these dreams was 'a *fake-world*, cleverly imitated but with small failures'. For example, in one lucid dream he tried the experiment of breaking a claret glass. In spite of hitting it with all his might the glass remained stubbornly intact, yet when he 'looked at it again after some time, it was broken...It broke all right but a little too late, like an actor missing his cue.'

In other words, in the world of the lucid dream, things are rarely quite what they seem. I remember in a lucid dream finding myself in a strange street in a strange town. Everything was apparently normal, as in any normal street. There were shops, there were people; the only abnormal thing was that, unlike everyone else, I was involuntarily gliding along several centimetres above the pavement instead of using my feet. At first I wondered if other people would notice, then realised I appeared to be invisible to them. As I passed two girls, something that trailed behind me, like a silk scarf, brushed against their faces, and they looked up puzzled and a little startled, as if half aware of a presence, yet unable to see what it was.

This and others of my lucid dreams illustrate the point I made earlier, namely that although one knows one is dreaming, the final decisions are still in the hands of the dream itself. Lucid dreams, for all the conscious clarity with which one experiences them, follow the logic of the dream world rather than the logic of waking life. So in my dream I found myself invisible to passers-by. My strong impression in the dream was that I was visiting some place that has objective existence, but I was there not as my waking self but in some kind of travelling, non-material body. The place I was visiting was obeying the laws of waking life, it was I who was breaking them.

For some dreamers, there is an experience similar to lucid dreaming which we call *false awakening*. Instead of becoming aware that the dream is a dream, the dreamer dreams that he or she awakes – sometimes to the point of actually believing they are dressing, or are at the breakfast table telling the family about the dreams of the night. Thus the dreamer almost gains consciousness within the dream, but instead of the consciousness registering the fact of dreaming, it makes 'sense' of the experience by assuming it is fully awake. People who experience false awakenings are sometimes able to go on and develop the condition into full lucid dreaming, using the technique I discuss on page 128. At other times they find the experience frightening. For example, in my own records I have the case of a woman who experienced a false awakening, and sat at the mirror to comb her hair, only to realise there was no reflection of her face in it. She looked down at her hands, and they weren't there either.

Out of the Body Experiences

Just as false awakening may be a half-way stage towards lucid dreaming, so lucid dreams appear to be a half-way stage between normal dreaming and OBEs (out-of-the-body experiences). In an OBE one travels through familiar and unfamiliar scenery just as in a lucid dream, but the difference is that one is aware of what seems to be an actual physical separation from one's body.

OBEs can happen at times other than sleep; for example as a result of a sudden shock to the body, or when unconscious under anaesthetic, or when the heart has stopped beating and one is for a short time clinically dead (a so-called NDE or near-death experience). The literature on the subject is a vast and rapidly growing one, and to launch into it would take us too far from dreaming. But experiences in dream OBEs seem to all intents and purposes to be the same as those that happen during these non-dreaming states, so for present purposes we can talk about dreaming and non-dreaming OBEs as if they are a single category.

So realistic is the feeling during an OBE that one is inhabiting a consciousness separate from one's physical body that one has the sensation of looking at the body from the outside, and may even struggle to re-enter it, fearing that death has occurred. For example, the first time I heard of an OBE (and there was very little available on them in those days) was in late adolescence, when the brother of a friend of mine while living in Egypt 'woke' to find himself suspended a metre or so above his sleeping body. In panic he struggled to, in his own words, 'get back on the bed', feeling convinced that if he failed to do so he would die. After a long struggle he was suddenly and violently projected back onto the bed, where he found himself pouring with sweat and his heart beating wildly.

The sense of realism in an OBE is often heightened by the fact that one can even notice things about the physical body that can't normally be seen while within it. For example, in another case from my own records, one of my students experienced an OBE while very ill and in a state of physical collapse. She saw herself placed on the stretcher and taken out of her house to the ambulance, and registered with a kind of detached interest 'Oh, so *that's* what my head and my hairstyle look like from the top!' Other people report similar experiences. Sometimes of floating along behind their physical bodies while out walking, and of seeing themselves from the back. Sometimes of seeing things that others are doing to them (a common experience during clinical death, when after recovery the patient sometimes describes to doctors and nurses elements of the treatment he or she received which apparently they could not have known by normal means).

Many spiritual and occult traditions have long taught that in OBEs the soul or astral body (call it what you will) actually does leave the physical body, and is free to travel both in this world and in the astral realms, and recent medical research into NDEs lends support to at least the first part of this conviction. Some authorities doubt it however, and claim the OBE is simply the way the imagination works under certain unusual sets of circumstances. Without entering too closely into this debate, my own approach is to ask people how OBE experiences seemed to them at the time, before the rational mind had a chance to step in and try to make 'sense' of them. There are dangers in insisting too swiftly that the experiences people have are not what they themselves take them to be. Where experiences are deeply personal, the subject's own interpretation of them isn't necessarily inferior to that of the 'expert' trying to rationalise them away from the outside.

If we ask people to interpret their own OBEs, they often express the conviction that the experience was exactly what it appeared to be. Namely that some part of their consciousness left the physical body and located outside it. In this sense, the OBE is in contrast both with ordinary dreams and lucid dreams. No matter how realistic the dream, we are sure on waking that it was only a dream. Whereas after the OBE the feeling remains, often undimmed years later, that consciousness can exist outside the physical body, and that the knowledge of this fact changes one's beliefs about both the nature of life and the nature of death.

Occult traditions have always maintained that each person's consciousness leaves the body during sleep (in other words, that we all have OBEs), and that dreams are dim fragments of this experience, filtered back through consciousness so that only confused memories are left instead of a clear awareness of actually leaving the physical body. Some light is perhaps thrown on this belief by one of my own experiences. Over a long period I had been aware of waking from time to time in the night with a puzzled, uneasy awareness of a particular corner of my bedroom. Trying to rationalise it to myself each time (not easy in the small hours of the morning) I assumed I must be having recurring dreams of someone standing in that corner and watching me.

One night I awoke from this experience with sufficient determination to try and recall the dream itself. I focused upon my awareness of that particular corner of the room, and at once clearly (and to my complete surprise) recalled the experience of having moments earlier been out of my body and up near the ceiling, looking down at the corner of the room in question. As with dreams themselves, there is no way of proving that this recall was accurate. But an interesting sidelight upon it is that the experience of waking with that particular kind of awareness ceased from that night on. It is as if the conscious mind is satisfied with the explanation, and no longer feels the sense of puzzled unease that prompted me to awake.

Lucid Dreams and OBEs

As to the connection between lucid dreams and OBEs, in one of my first experiences of lucid dreams I told myself that I wanted to fly. I was immediately and to my great surprise thrown on my back and propelled, head first and at great speed, through a black space, like a very dark night. At the same moment I heard a rushing, roaring noise inside my head and my whole body vibrated (inwardly rather than physically) at a very high frequency. It was the first time I had experienced the phenomenon, but I found myself saying, still asleep; 'I know what's going to happen; I'm going to leave my body.' Though not particularly frightened, I thought it sensible to say a prayer for protection. The instant I did so, as if a switch had been thrown, the experience ended.

Checking up later I found I was correct in recognising that the rushing noise and the feeling of vibration are reported by many writers as a frequent prelude to an OBE. Four of the leading writers on OBEs all describe it, either from first-hand experience or from records compiled from the experiences of others. Muldoon talks about a feeling throughout his whole body of a 'vibration at a great rate of speed, in an up–and–down direction', while Monroe talks of 'vibrations' or 'tingles', rather like 'an electric shock', and Crookall reports a correspondent who experienced 'a roar or low frequency vibration …through my whole body'. Walker also describes this experience, pointing out, as does Muldoon, that 'this uncontrollable shaking is not apparently connected with the physical body, which remains motionless throughout'.

I had read these accounts some years before having the experience I described a moment ago, but had completely forgotten them at a conscious level. The most striking feature of the experience was therefore its total unexpectedness. In asking to fly in the lucid dream, I had expected nothing more than a gentle wafting over the dream scenery in front of me, not an OBE and certainly not the rather awesome prelude to it. (As to the way in which the prayer for safety ended the experience, I can only offer this as indication that even in dreams prayer seems a rather powerful business.)

Inducing Lucid Dreams

Since lucid dreams have such a special quality about them, people naturally ask if there are ways in which they can be deliberately induced. The answer is that there are helpful techniques, but as in other dreamwork, patience is the watchword. You may practise a technique for weeks, months on end with no sign you're any nearer your goal. And then suddenly and unexpectedly, one night it happens. Keep the mind light, almost playful, as if you don't really care whether you lucid dream or not, you're simply mildly curious about it. Treated this way, rather as the poet woos the shy creative muse, you make success more likely.

The first technique is meditation. There are many systems of meditation, but the principle underpinning them all is that they give the mind a point of focus (Box 10). Instead of dashing madly backwards and forwards after this thought and then that as usual, the mind is held on an object of concentration, whether it be the breath, a mantra, a visualisation or whatever. Through practising in this way the mind becomes calmer and stiller,

BOX 10
MEDITATION

Meditation is a major subject in its own right, and I've space only to touch on one or two of the issues that help most with our dreaming. The benefits of meditation at both psychological and spiritual levels are many and far-reaching. From the point of view of dreaming the most important of these are that the regular practice of meditation (daily if possible):

* improves concentration, thus allowing you to be more aware during both waking and sleeping of what is going on in your own mind

* improves access to your unconscious.

Meditation Techniques

A short period of meditation last thing at night is one of the best ways of giving you more access to your creativity, and in particular to the creative world of dreams. Choose as quiet a place as possible, and sit on an upright chair or cross-legged on the floor. To begin with, five minutes meditation is enough. As your practice progresses, so you will find this period tends to extend of its own accord until it stretches to 20 minutes or so. Lower the eyelids so that you are aware of only a narrow band of unfocused light, or close your eyes completely if you prefer (and can still keep awake).

The aim in meditation is to keep the mind alert yet relaxed, and focused upon a single stimulus rather than upon the ceaseless chatter of your thoughts. A good stimulus to choose is your breathing. Put your awareness in the gentle rise and fall of your abdomen, or at the place in your nostrils where you feel the air cool as you breathe in and warm as you breathe out. Count each out breath silently from one to 10, and when you get to 10 go back again to one. If you lose track of your counting, go back to one each time. Don't try to push away the thoughts that arise during this practice, but don't attend to them and don't follow them. Let each one enter and leave the mind while you concentrate upon the breathing.

An alternative point of focus is the point just above and between the eyes, the 'third eye' of yoga philosophy, and it helps if you can visualise a white light here.

As you practise meditation regularly and as your concentration improves, you can place at your point of concentration the idea that your consciousness will flow easily and smoothly from waking into sleep. Repeat this as a formula of words if you like, though if you can it's better to hold it as

---

BOX 10
MEDITATION

an abstract idea, or like the idea of a journey that flows
smoothly and uninterruptedly from waking through sleep and
into reawaking tomorrow morning.
    When you finish the meditation, keep the mind in this calm
and tranquil state. It's best to go straight to bed. Keep your
physical movements unhurried, as if they are flowing in
harmony with your consciousness. When you settle to sleep,
allow your awareness to rest gently in the same place as your
meditation.

---

more aware of what is going on within it, and therefore better
able to know the difference between waking and sleeping
consciousness.

Some of the improved powers of concentration which come
from meditation seem thus to carry over into sleep itself, and to
help with the second technique, which is to train yourself to
recognise the anomalies and illogicalities which occur in
dreaming. Once you recognise these anomalies instead of
accepting them without question (as we usually do in
dreaming), you reach the point of recognising 'Ah, so this must
be a dream!' And it is this recognition which is one of the main
ways of launching yourself into lucid dreaming.

For example, in one of my lucid dreams I was standing in a
busy shopping street in what I knew for some reason was
Britain, but when I looked at the names above the shops I saw
they were in French. At once the realisation dawned on me,
with that start of excitement which always comes at the
beginning of a lucid dream, that anomalies such as French
names above all the shops in a British high street only occur in
dreams, and that therefore I was adrift in the dream world.

On another occasion I was 'time-travelling' in a dream, and
for some reason was back to the 1930s, meeting the South
African cricket team then touring Britain. (When I told one of
the team I was time-travelling he showed only mild interest, as
if there was nothing special about that.) The sudden realisation
that time–travelling could only happen in dreams made the
dream become lucid, but I was so enjoying the time–travelling
that I debated with myself whether to let the dream carry on in

a non-lucid state, or whether to plump for lucidity. In the end I plumped for lucidity.

The alertness needed to recognise the strangeness of the goings-on in a dream and therefore to realise we're dreaming seems so easy to our daytime mind, yet once asleep we accept the most bizarre and unlikely happenings as a commonplace. So to lucid dream, we must find ways of carrying some of our daytime alertness into sleep. As I've just said, a few minutes meditation, in which the mind observes its own mental processes, helps. But a second technique is to ask yourself as often as possible during the day how you know you're not dreaming *now*. This instant.

How do you know? Is it because things happen predictably? You turn on the tap and water flows; you look out of the window and see the expected scenery; you put things down and they stay in the same place. Or is it because objects remain stable instead of undergoing strange metamorphoses? A book remains a book instead of changing into a cushion; a landscape remains a landscape instead of changing into a seascape. Or is it because you can take decisions and carry them out? You decide to run and your legs obey you; you decide to speak and words emerge. Is it because you aren't constantly doing odd things like flying, or shooting people, or appearing nude in public?

By frequent reality testing of this kind, you train your mind to be more aware when things don't behave as they should, with the result that you leave yourself better equipped to notice the tell-tale unreality of the dream.

A third technique is to tell yourself, as you go off to sleep, that you're going to recognise your dreams for what they are. Repeat over and over again a set formula of words such as 'I'll know that I'm dreaming', and at the same time *imagine* yourself knowing this. Imagine yourself looking objectively at dream events, spotting the anomalies and realising exactly what is going on. Help yourself further by thinking, during the day, of your consciousness as a continuous process stretching over the 24 hours instead of suspending itself during sleep. In this way you come to see waking events and dream events as parts of a continuum, rather than as separate categories of experience. A continuum in which you remain as attentive and aware during sleeping as during waking.

Muldoon, an important writer on out-of-the-body experiences, advocated a somewhat similar method which involved retaining consciousness for as long as possible into the hypnogogic state, and then imagining a dream for yourself that contains the idea of rising up out of your body. For example, floating up to the surface of a pond, or climbing a ladder, or going up in a lift. When you've risen as high as you can go, simply step out or off and find yourself in a lucid dream or even in an out–of–the–body experience.

A fourth technique is to give yourself a task to do somewhere in the house while you're asleep, and focus your mind upon it during the day and last thing at night. One exercise I use in dream workshops is to tell participants to request someone at home to write down four numbers on a piece of paper for them, seal it in an envelope, and place it conspicuously on a table downstairs. When dreaming, the task is to go downstairs, open the envelope and read the number.

I often angle the task towards ESP. There is no sense in which (unless they are sleepwalking) they will be able actually to open the physical envelope. But they might, in dreams, be able to open a kind of ESP equivalent of the envelope and read the contents. From an ESP point of view, the main problem is that although some individuals do indeed find the envelope and read the number in dreams, unless they are awakened there and then – as in a dream laboratory – the memory of the number is too vague to be much use the following morning. (Though Fox, an early writer on the subject, claims that he saw and remembered two of the questions on an important examination paper when lucid dreaming.) But from the point of view of lucid dreaming, the exercise often produces rapid results. For example, on only the third night of trying this method, one dreamer reported that:

> I found myself standing in the back garden, looking up at the house. I knew there was something inside the house that I had to find, and as I remembered that I had to find it in dreams I realised I must be dreaming. The house looked just as usual, only I think it was bigger or I was smaller. It was night-time, and the sky was full of very bright stars. I told myself I must go into the house, and the next thing I knew I was in a tunnel of stars, and I thought 'This must be the way into the house.' At that point, I lost the dream and started to dream non-lucidly about something else.

After a similarly short period, another dreamer reported that:

> I was walking along the landing, and although it was night-time I could see clearly, so I knew I must be dreaming. I seemed to float down the stairs and found my way easily into the dining room. The envelope was on the table, but I found I couldn't pick it up. The next moment I had it in my hand. There was something inside, but when I looked at it I could see marks on the paper but couldn't read them.

A variant on this technique, which again employs the notion of a task, is to leave a glass of drinking water in the bathroom, and then eat very salty food before retiring. In the night one feels thirsty but, since the body is reluctant to awake and actually go to the bathroom, the journey there becomes incorporated into a dream, and the awareness that this is happening reminds one that a dream is taking place. Another variant is to drink plenty of liquid so that in the night one wants to get up and empty the bladder; again the journey is done in a dream, and brings the realisation that a dream is taking place. There's no evidence, by the way, that this makes you any more likely to wet the bed. But it's hardly a pleasant method, although I have found that it can work for me, though in a rather fragmented way.

Sometimes we realise we're dreaming for reasons other than a recognition of the strangeness of the dream world. For example, in one of my dreams I was standing in the street looking up at the wording written around a clock face in the tower of a stone building. Finding myself able to read the words I thought to myself 'That's funny, usually in dreams you can't read things', and this was enough to prompt me to realise that 'yes, of course, this is a dream!'. On another occasion I was (for some obscure reason) hanging onto the sill of an upstairs window and in imminent danger of falling. Then the realisation came to me 'It's only a dream; so you can let go.' (I did so and floated pleasantly down.)

People trying to break free of nightmares (page 98) often find that putting into effect the advice to turn around and face whatever it is that's pursuing them prompts lucidity. So does putting into practice the advice to wonder *why* their legs won't carry them when they're trying to escape a pursuer. And the advice that guns, knives, fists or whatever can't really hurt them. Other people find that repeating as often as possible, during the day and last thing at night, a phrase such as 'My dreams are my own invention and I can do what I like with them', helps lucidity right from the outset of many of their dreams.

A technique used by American Indians which also relies upon sharpened concentration in waking life is to close your eyes and regularly try and visualise your hands. Tell yourself as you do so that you will see your hands in your dream, and that when you do you will know you are dreaming.

One final technique. When remembering your dreams each morning, look for illogicalities. Ask yourself why these weren't enough to tell you that you were dreaming. Convince yourself that next time these sorts of things will be quite enough to make you realise you're dreaming. The more familiar you become with your dream world, the more likely you are to recognise it for what it is and allow it to become lucid. Look at your dreams objectively. In my work with dreamers, I find paradoxically that those who dismiss their dreams as 'rubbish' or 'nonsense' are far less likely to have ever experienced lucid dreams than those who approach their dreams as if they have a special kind of reality.

The point about viewing dreams as if they have this kind of 'reality' is that it helps you view them while they're happening with some of the same powers of judgement you use in waking life. If you're constantly telling yourself your dreams are rubbish, your conscious mind seems happy to leave it at that and not to bother about them when they're taking place. Remind yourself instead that in waking life reality is not just the external world but the sense we make of it inside our own heads. We are the actors in our own story and the directors and often the authors and the audience as well. Much the same is true of dreams, and there is no reason why the *way* we make sense of waking life can't be carried over into dreaming.

Help matters further by reflecting upon your dreams with the same quality of mind you use to reflect upon waking events. Run them through in your mind, like any other set of memories. Try and recall the *texture* of them, not simply the events themselves. Tell yourself that in future dreams you must revisit the places remembered from past dreams, in just the way you can revisit places in waking life. Own your dreams, in the way you own the rest of your experience.

Integrating your dreaming into your waking life has other benefits beside the encouragement of lucid dreaming, of course, and these are returned to in the next chapter, where we look at how you can make use of dreams to help your spiritual growth and to face the profounder issues which life holds for us.

8

DREAMING
OF OTHER WORLDS

I referred in Chapter 1 to the importance attached to dreams in the great spiritual traditions of the world. So great an importance, in fact, that it's strange that modern religious thinking has now turned its back so firmly on the dream experience.

Or I should say modern *Western* religious thinking. Particularly in the religions influenced by the ancient shamanic cultures of central Asia, Africa and the Americas, dreams are still treated with the utmost respect. And nowhere more so than in the teachings of Tibetan Buddhism, especially the teachings known as Highest Yoga Tantra. For the practitioner of these teachings, sleep and dreaming provide us with nothing less than a dress rehearsal for death. Master sleep and dreams, and instead of being carried along at death and in the immediate after-death state (the bardo state) as a stream carries a leaf, you are on the way to shaping your own destiny. To the Tibetan Buddhist, shaping your own destiny means choosing your path through the bardo world, and deciding for yourself where and when to be reborn.

It would trivialise the enormous richness of the Tibetan teaching to suggest that this power of choice depends solely upon the degree of control with which you die. Your actions in this life also play a major part, and in fact ultimately determine the extent to which you are able to gain this kind of control. Unless you have cultivated compassion to all beings, and realised in meditation the true nature of existence (the emptiness from which the world of appearance arises) and of your own self, the achievement of these practices will be beyond you.

But conversely, if you have done these three things and yet not achieved these practices and learnt how to die, you will be helpless to shape events in the bardo state. You will certainly, through the great merit gained in this life, be reborn in the heavenly realms, there to live in bliss for aeons. But one day this merit will be exhausted, and return to this world will then become inevitable. Only in this world, by mastering death as well as life, can you escape from the rule of karma, from the wheel of cause and effect, and become free to shape your own existence.

In the Highest Yoga Tantra teachings, we are told we pass through no less than eight stages as we make our journey through death, and we need to learn how to remain conscious up until the seventh of them. These stages translate into English as:

Mirages
Smoke
Fireflies
Butter-lamp flame
Radiant white sky
Radiant red sky
Radiant black sky
Clear light

The first state, that of mirages, is equivalent to the hypnogogic state (Chapter 4). In it we see visions of our past life, of our hopes and longings, perhaps of the 'scenery' of other worlds, of loved ones already dead. The second stage is an awareness of what is described as resembling blue puffs of smoke billowing from a chimney against a smokey background. In the third stage, burning red sparks appear in the smoke, and in the fourth stage there is a spluttering flame, like a butter lamp about to go out. The fifth stage is marked by an awareness of extreme clarity and openness in a white light like 'a night sky pervaded by moonlight in the autumn when the sky is free from defilement'. In the sixth stage, clarity and openness increase further in a red or orange light 'like an autumn sky free of defilement and pervaded by sunlight', while in the seventh stage the awareness is of blackness 'like an autumn sky free of defilement and pervaded by a thick blackness like the beginning of night'.

In the final, eighth stage the clear light comes, 'like the natural colour of a dawn sky in autumn, free even of the ''pollutions'' of moonlight, sunlight and darkness. This is the clear light of death.'

In this precise mapping of the death-bed experience, we see the mind moving by eight stages from a coarse to an increasingly subtle state. The first four stages are the stages of 'signs' (or forms), the last four the stages of 'emptiness' (pure creative essence without attributes). The first three of the empty stages are not entirely empty however. Vestiges of forms still persist in that the mind continues to see a distinction between itself and the rest of reality – the mind on the one hand and the resemblance to 'moonlight', 'sunlight', and 'darkness' on the other. But at the end of the stage of darkness there comes a moment of unconsciousness when the mind relinquishes the last of this dualism, to re-emerge in the eighth stage into an experience of supreme reality (the unity of all things) in the clear light of death.

The teachings tell us that one usually remains in this state of clear light for some three days after death (during which time it is emphasised that the body should be allowed to remain undisturbed), after which one passes through the eight stages in reverse order (thus passing from subtlety back into coarseness), and is then reborn in the intermediate world (the bardo), where one once more possesses a body, and where one wanders through other-world scenery searching for a place to be reborn.

If a suitable place isn't found, one undergoes another death (described as a 'small death') during which the eight stages of death are once more experienced, but this time only fleetingly. They are followed by the same eight stages in reverse order, and by another period in the intermediate world looking for a place in which to be reborn. This cycle of 'small deaths' and 'rebirths' can take place up to seven times in the intermediate state, after which one necessarily leaves the intermediate state and is reborn, but by now without real choice as to place or to parents.

The more spiritually advanced the individual, the better his or her chance of finding a suitable rebirth out of the intermediate state. This rebirth can be in a spirit body or back into a human body, the latter being preferable even to rebirth in the heavenly realms since it is only in a human body that one can achieve final enlightenment (or the rebirth can be in one of the inferior or 'hell' realms, but that is another story). One's attitude of mind at the point of death is also important. If even a spiritually advanced person dies in a state of anger or desire or any other negative emotion, this will have an adverse effect upon their experiences in the bardo state.

The aim of the very advanced practitioner, however, is to remain within the clear light of death, instead of relinquishing it and re-entering the cycle of existence through the reverse process of the eight stages of dying. If he or she is unable to remain within this clear light the first time it appears, there are further chances during the 'small deaths' that happen in the bardo state, but since these are progressively more and more fleeting, the opportunity becomes more and more difficult to grasp.

For those who are able to remain within the clear light, rebirth takes place not in the world of forms but in the formless realm of infinite space. This is the realm (in as much as it can be described in human terms) of infinite consciousness, of nothingness (no-thing-ness), the peak of cyclic existence from where one has infinite freedom of choice. Choice which encompasses being reborn in this world with the sole aim of helping others (the Bodhisattva ideal) or of passing on to ultimate Nirvana, a state about which nothing can be said, so far is it beyond our human comprehension.

This rather lengthy description of the after-death state is essential if we are to understand how sleep and dreams are seen in the Tantric teaching as a dress rehearsal for death. The teaching tells us that sleep is akin to the 'small deaths' that occur in the bardo state. We pass through each of the eight stages in the first hour or so of sleep, culminating in the clear light which precedes the onset of dreaming. The trouble is that usually we're not aware of them (we're said to pass through them also in orgasm and in fainting, though awareness is even less likely at these times!). The result is that we have no more control over our dreams than we will one day have over the intermediate state and our next rebirths.

So slight, in fact, is our control over our consciousness during these eight stages, that we struggle even to remain conscious during the first of them, the stage of mirages which we call the hypnogogic state. Tantra is the practice of transformation, the transformation of our gross psychological and physical states into more subtle, spiritual ones. So instead of animalistic slumber during the hours of sleep, Tantra tells us that the mind should transmute into a higher state of consciousness in which it remains alert and aware, and free in the sense that it has choice over what happens when it enters the world of dreaming.

The experience of lucid dreaming (Chapter 7) appears to be an emergence into this awareness and freedom, but a fragmented and capricious emergence, probably at only a low level of consciousness, rather in the way that a sodden piece of wood sluggishly breaks surface in the current of a rushing river, only to disappear again a moment later.

Whether it is possible, without undergoing long and intensive Tantric training, ever to 'purify' the mind to the point where we gain proper control over the processes of our own being, remains doubtful. My own experiences with Tantric teachers suggests that, however we approach it, the task is likely to be a long and difficult one, involving not only enormous dedication and effort but also a fundamental shift in the way in which we think about existence and our own place within it.

But simply knowing about the states identified in Highest Yoga Tantra is a help, and assists us in making an initial change in perspective. We can go a little further and also know a little about some of the practices that render one conscious of these states. Elements of these practices can be introduced into our work on sleep and dreaming, though it would be wrong to suppose that over-simplifications of this kind take us into the real heart of Highest Yoga Tantra teachings.

The rationale behind these practices is that the four empty stages that we experience during dying and during sleep represent the process of seeing beyond the world of forms and into the world of infinite potential (emptiness) from which the world of forms arises. To experience them, we must remain conscious as they unfold before us in sleep. In the Tantric teaching, each of the four stages (the stages of forms) that precede the four empty stages is marked by a particular type of disengagement from the outside world. In the stage of mirages, we lose the ability to open our eyes, in the stage of smoke we lose awareness of external sounds, in the stage of fireflies we lose the sense of smell, and in the butter-lamp stage we lose the sense of taste. In other words, our awareness becomes gradually dislocated from our senses and is able to exist in and of itself, at a subtle level. For most of us, operating as we do at a crude level of being, this loss of contact with the senses means that we lose consciousness altogether, because for us consciousness is simply something that registers sensory experience and expresses itself through speech, and very little more.

But to the practitioner, even without sense data and speech, consciousness remains. In the four stages of emptiness, his or her mind becomes divorced even from thoughts, and exists in its own subtle essence, the process reaching completion in the eighth stage when the clear light dawns.

Little research has been carried out in the West into the way in which consciousness progressively withdraws from the senses during the initial stages of sleep. The obvious way of doing this research would be to experiment with attempting to wake the sleeper first by a bright light, then by sounds, then by smells, and finally by taste. If the teachings of Highest Yoga Tantra are correct, early on we'll be able to arouse the sleeper by all four stimuli, but he or she will then become responsive only to the three last, then the two last, then to only the last, and finally to none of the four.

Since these teachings are about subtlety not about grossness, each of the stimuli would have to be presented in a subdued rather than an intrusive form. If we make a loud enough noise any sleeper will awake, no matter what stage of sleep he or she has reached. However, if the teachings are correct, the further the sleeper has progressed beyond the stage when he or she is easily rousable by a given stimulus, the more distress and confusion they will experience if we exaggerate the stimulus until it finally breaks through into their consciousness.

But to return to the practice itself. I have already talked about remaining conscious in the first stage of sleeping, the hypnogogic stage or the stage of mirages (Chapter 4). To remain conscious in the next three stages, we need some simple props to help us. Most of us have had the experience, as we start to doze in the living room, of that moment when the murmer of voices or of the television becomes far away. We're conscious of them receding from our awareness. This is, in fact, the second stage of sleeping. So if we have in the bedroom the gentle ticking of a clock or the soft sound of taped music we can focus on maintaining awareness as the sound becomes faint and ultimately disappears. This allows us to stay aware into this second stage.

Scent of some kind in the bedroom (incense, pot-pourri) helps us in the third stage, while a strong taste in the mouth (garlic, bitter aloes, even a mint-flavoured toothpaste) helps us in the fourth. As with sound, the practice is to remain aware of the moment when we can no longer smell the scent, no longer taste the taste. Beyond this fourth stage, the stage of taste, only personal experience can assist you. There's little further I can say.

For the reader who wonders why simply focusing upon lucid dreams isn't enough, without bothering about these earlier stages, I have to say that the practices I'm now talking about take us much further. Tantric teachings are about transformation, the transformation of negative emotions into positive, of physical energy into spiritual. But only Highest Yoga Tantra is about transforming the death state itself, transforming not only our condition in this world but in worlds to come as well. For the materially minded who don't want to venture into such contentious issues as what (if anything) survives physical death, this transformation can be seen as the transformation of consciousness from its present, fragmented, incomplete state into a continuous, unified experience that opens up our full potential of mind and being. A transformation from partiality into wholeness, from psychological immaturity into psychological maturity.

In this sense then, Highest Yoga Tantra is the most profound of all the psychological teachings on the subject of sleep and dreams. And although sleep and dreaming are largely private states, this teaching is in no sense a 'selfish' one, or divorced from other people and the concerns of this life. Through working on our sleep and dreams we are working on ourselves at the deepest level of our being, and it is taught that by doing this we naturally become more compassionate, more understanding and more loving towards our fellows. As we realise, through this practice, more and more of our full potential as human beings, we free ourselves from the prison of our conditioning and allow ourselves to experience our lives and the lives of others in the fullest and most rewarding way.

Which seems a noble enough reason for taking the practice seriously.

Dream Visits

I mentioned in Chapter 2 that in some of the Eastern traditions it is claimed that pupil and master (or any two people sharing a close bond) can visit each other at will in dreams, with both aware the following morning that the visit has taken place. Once one has control of one's dreams, as in lucid dreaming and as discussed in the last section, such visits seem more credible. In the course of the lucid dream, one 'wills' oneself to the required place, and in theory that should be that.

In practice, I find that isn't necessarily that at all. People report variously that they seem not to arrive precisely where they want to be, or that they see the person they want to visit but are unable to attract their attention, or (more usually) that somewhere along the way they lose lucidity and slip back into ordinary dreaming. For these reasons, I haven't personally come across a case where, using lucid dreams alone, both dreamers were aware of the visit and were each able the following morning to corroborate the other's version of it.

But I have talked to lamas trained in Highest Yoga Tantra who, using the practices I've just been discussing, assure me they themselves have experienced these dream visits. Their ingrained reticence about talking of their inner experiences ('If you are interested in such things, then you must practise until you attain them for yourself') means I can't question them as closely as I would like, and have to take some part of what they tell me on trust. But in the light of what I know about such men and women, trust isn't difficult to come by.

Western Traditions

However, in the Western parapsychological literature there are several recorded cases of individuals willing themselves to visit a friend while in the waking or sleeping state. The following day, confirmation has come from the friend that, without knowing about the experiment, the experimenter appeared to them so clearly they thought he or she was there in the flesh. Typically the experimenter has no knowledge of seeing the other person and may not even recall a lucid dream, so he or she is unaware of the success of the enterprise until this confirmation is received.

A typical technique used (very similar to that employed by Western occult traditions) involves:

1. putting the mind into a 'neutral' state, as in meditation.

2. holding an image of the other person in the mind and preferably building up a clear, strong visualisation of him or her (knowledge of the setting in which you want to see them also helps).

3. concentrating, lightly but persistently, upon being with the other person, on 'feeling' you are with them as well as 'seeing' yourself there.

4. holding this concentration as you drift into sleep or into a state of deep reverie.

I find this practice works best if the other person knows what I'm trying to do (though without necessarily knowing the exact time I'm doing it) and is in a receptive state. But the real test of whether their awareness of me is real or imaginary would be to visit them when they know nothing of my intention (in which case they would have to note exactly when and where they became conscious of me – something they would be unlikely to do if they have no prior warning I want them to do this), or to convey a test message of some kind to them which they have no way of knowing by normal means.

You are in as good a position to carry out tests of this kind as am I or anyone else. If you try out the technique, the ground rules are much as already given in connection with other dreamwork. Firstly don't try too hard. Success depends more upon motivation, concentration, and the clarity of one's visualisations than upon sheer will-power. And secondly, don't be impatient. Success, if it comes, may take weeks or months of steady, regular effort.

But is this all the Western traditions have to offer in this area of dreamwork? Not quite. Highest Yoga Tantra has no direct parallel in the West but, in certain relevant respects, alchemy comes close to it. Remember that Tantra is about transforming our negative or undeveloped qualities; so indeed is alchemy. Far from being a set of quaint superstitions on turning base metal into gold, what the alchemist tried to transform was the 'base metal' of the self, and the thing into which he tried to transform it was the 'gold' of pure essence, the source ('emptiness') from which all existence springs.

So spiritual rather than material wealth was the alchemist's prime aim. And although alchemical treatises make little direct mention of dreams, they are full of images and symbols which provide striking analogies with those in dreams and visions. Jung gives us extensive examples of these, and considers they show that both in dreams and alchemical practices the same deep strata of the unconscious is contacted.

At this deep strata (the strata where in Jungian psychology our individual, separate unconscious mind merges into the unifying collective unconscious) we each carry the divine spark, the higher self, the universal soul, call it what you will. Jung has it that alchemy teaches us that our task as humans is to deliver this divine essence from its slumbers. Instead of relying for salvation upon some divinity *outside* ourselves, alchemy teaches that it is we who are the actual saviours of divinity *within*.

By studying the images and symbols in the alchemical texts and in dreams and visions we come into closer communion with this divine essence. Jung tells us to use these symbols as our focus of concentration in meditation, to make drawings of them, to visualise them. By so doing, we draw closer together our conscious and our unconscious minds, until we reach the point of wholeness where they remain in communion with each other.

Alchemical texts strongly suggest consciousness can be continuous between waking and sleeping, and that progress can be made towards this continuity while awake as well as when asleep. The same view is taken by other Western magical traditions. The magician, through the power of his or her creative imagination, is allegedly able to do all the things one can do in a dream, but do them consciously and intentionally. The creative imagination in waking life and not just in dreaming is the doorway to other worlds. First one trains this imagination so that one can visualise, clearly and steadily (visualisation has always been a central part of the training both of the Eastern spiritual acolyte and of the Western sorcerer's apprentice), then one actually enters and travels in this world of one's own creation.

And yet not of one's own creation. Because by visualising the symbols given in the alchemical and magical texts one ensures that the magical world one enters has an objective reality. The symbols are not just any old symbols. They are special ones, the keys to the magical world, and although when we visualise them initially they are the work of our own imagination, they allow us to tune in to this world and then become part of it. So much so in fact that the magician claims to be able to share the voyage into this world with fellow adepts, each person entering the same experiences, very much as in the dream visits I talked about earlier.

Israel Regardie, one of the leading authorities on Western magic, dismisses our usual fragmented dream experiences. Like the Tantric practitioner he lays great store upon remaining conscious throughout the night, and maintains that this state can be reached through alchemical and magical visualisation practices. As a result of these practices one no longer passes the night in what he calls 'deep oblivion or at best in the phantastic adventure of dream'. One passes it 'with the consciousness retained even during sleep. There is no long gap of oblivion: all is one continuous free-flowing stream of awareness.'

He goes on to tell us that 'The importance of this attainment cannot be overestimated...Consciousness of the highest Soul persists in every hour.' Even 'death is transcended', as the magician attains the certainty that only the body, mind and emotions die, and that the Soul remains 'serene and imperturbable in the knowledge of its own Immortality'.

Impressive stuff. This insistence from both Eastern and Western esoteric traditions upon the importance of retaining consciousness throughout sleep should surely set us all thinking.

Conclusion

How you see dreams is in the end a matter for you. Whether as the meaningless product of random brain activity, as an enchanted voyage into your own imagination, as a method for solving psychological problems, or as a route towards spiritual unfoldment. My advice to those who want final answers to the meaning and purpose of dreams is that they must put these questions to their own dreaming minds. The best that anyone else can do for them is to introduce them to the techniques they need in order to listen to these answers. As in so many areas of human psychology and spirituality, true understanding comes only at the level of personal experience. The message over the door that leads nightly into your dreams bids you watch, take note, take part, and learn. The more closely you do this, the more aware you will become of what dreaming is for, and that there is no sharp divide between waking and sleeping, no insurmountable barrier that decrees these two parts of our existence must for ever remain separate. You will discover that dreaming is as much an element of our mental lives as are our waking moments.

ENDWORD

Certain questions arise time and time again when readers and callers to phone-in programmes ask me for information about dreaming. I will conclude by looking at the three most frequent topics.

The first one concerns recurring dreams. People of all ages report having the same dream over and over again, often over a period of many years, and they wonder if there is any particular significance in this. The answer is yes, for two main reasons. The first is that recurring dreams further weaken the argument (examined and disposed of in Chapter 1) that dreams are merely a consequence of the brain's dumping unwanted material during sleep, rather as computers discard unwanted information when we exit from a program. Recurring dreams clearly indicate that the material concerned is not 'unwanted', and relates to issues firmly established in the mind.

The second reason for the significance of recurring dreams is that they indicate there are matters deserving particular attention in the dreamer's psychological life. The dream is repeatedly attempting to draw attention to these matters, perhaps because they have to do with an area of life or of psychological potential that the dreamer is neglecting, or because they relate to old anxieties or concerns that have not yet been laid to rest. Alternatively, the dream may be trying to provide guidance as to long-term life-goals, or the particular path that will prove best for the dreamer.

Interestingly, recurring dreams sometimes involve a place (typically a house) that the dreamer has never visited in waking life, but which is seen in such detail, and is so consistent in appearance, that the dreamer is haunted by a sense of its objective reality. Sometimes he or she may actually go searching for it when awake, and not surprisingly wonders if the dream could be precognitive, or perhaps an echo of a previous life. The answer is, of course, that recurring dreams are no less symbolic than ordinary dreams. The place (particularly if it is a house) may thus represent the dreamer, and the dream may be showing that there are large areas of the self that still remain to be discovered, or that for some reason the dreamer is not allowing the real self to be fully expressed. (Dream symbols, and in particular the tendency for houses to represent the dreamer's own self, are discussed in more detail in my book *The Secret Language of Dreams*.)

Another question that often crops up has to do with meeting in dreams people who are known to have died. Sometimes such people look exactly as the dreamer remembered them, at other times they seem younger, or more beautiful, or restored to full health and vigour. Sometimes they give messages, often of comfort and reassurance, concerning both their continuing existence, and the future wellbeing and happiness of the dreamer.

It is all too easy to dismiss these dreams as wishful thinking, particularly if the dreamer was close to the person who has died, and has experienced a strong sense of loss and sadness. But my question to the dreamer is always, 'How do *you* feel about the experience? It is your dream: what do *you* think was happening?' Such a question is highly relevant. It is absurd to suppose that modern man has somehow 'proved' there is no life after death. At worst we simply don't know whether life goes on after the death of the physical body, and at best we have some very suggestive evidence (from near-death experiences, from mediumistic communications, and from the teachings of the great spiritual traditions) that it does. Thus if the dreamer feels convinced that someone who has died was communicating in the dream, then this may very well be what was happening.

I am also sometimes asked about the devices currently coming on the market for inducing lucid dreams, and about whether they really work. The answer is that there is no guarantee. They function by noting those changes in breathing pattern or brain rhythms or eye movements that signal the sleeper has entered dreaming sleep, and they administer some small stimulus (such as a very mild electric shock) which is in theory sufficient to alert the dreamer to the fact that he or she is dreaming, but insufficient to produce awakening. For some people, this seems to be effective (although they may have to practise with the device for some weeks first); for others it is less so. The interested reader can learn more about this approach in K. Hearne's *The Dream Machine.* By all means try one of these devices if you like. They have been developed by serious scientists after careful research.

Ideally, however, lucid dreaming should arise spontaneously as the mind develops its powers through meditation and the other techniques covered in Chapter 7. There is a risk that a short cut into lucid dreaming could be nothing more than a device for making your dreamlife more exciting. Valuable as this may be, it may not lead to deeper levels of inner understanding. Lucid dreaming should at best be seen as a sign of psycho-spiritual progress, rather than as an end in itself.

It would be wrong to end by wishing you only sweet dreams. Dreams are part of life itself, and life inevitably contains its bitter moments as well as its sweet ones. It would be unrealistic to pretend otherwise. Let me end, however, by wishing you wisdom in your dreams and the patience in your waking life to follow the path of that wisdom.

REFERENCES AND
FURTHER READING

Blackmore, S. *Beyond the Body: An investigation of out-of-the-body experiences*, Paladin, 1983.

Boss, M. *I Dreamt Last Night*, Gardner Press, 1977.

Brook, S. *The Oxford Book of Dreams*, Oxford University Press, 1987.

Crookall, R. *More Astral Projections*, Aquarian, 1964.

Dunne, J. W. *An Experiment With Time*, Faber & Faber, 5th Edition, 1939.

Fontana, D. *The Secret Language of Dreams*, Pavilion Books (UK) and Chronicle (USA), 1994.

Fox, O. *Astral Projection*, University Books, 1962.

Freud, S. *The Interpretation of Dreams*, Penguin, 1976.

Garfield, P. G. *Creative Dreaming*, Futura, 1976.

Green, C. E. *Lucid Dreams*, Hamish Hamilton, 1968.

Gurney, E., Myers, F.W.H. and Podmore, F. *Phantasms of the Living* (2 vols.), Trübner, 1886.

Hearne, K. *The Dream Machine*, Aquarian Press, 1990.

Hobson, J. A. *Sleep*, Scientific American, 1989.

Horwood, H. *The Conquest of Time*, London: privately published by the author, 1959.

Hutin, S. *History of Alchemy*, Tower, 1962.

Jung, C. *Dream Analysis*, Routledge, 1984.

Mavromatis, A. *Hypnogogia: The unique state of consciousness between waking and sleeping*, Routledge, 1987.

Monroe, R. *Journeys Out of the Body*, Corgi, 1974.

Moody, R. and Perry, P. *The Light Beyond: The transforming power of Near Death Experiences*, Pan, 1989.

Muldoon, S. and Carrington, H. *The Projection of the Astral Body*, Rider, 3rd Edition, 1968.

Perls, F. *Gestalt Therapy Verbatim*, Bantam, 1971.

Regardie, I. *The Tree of Life: A study in magic*, Samuel Weiser, 1972.

Rinbochay, L. and Hopkins, J. *Death, Intermediate State and Re-birth in Tibetan Buddhism*, Snow Lion, 1980.

Ullman, M. and Zimmerman, N. *Working With Dreams*, Aquarian Press, 1987.

Walker, B. *Beyond the Body*, Routledge and Kegan Paul, 1977.

Van Eeden. F. 'A Study of dreams'. *Proceedings of the Society for Psychical Research*, Vol 26, 1913.

INDEX